797,885 Books
are available to read at

Forgotten Books

www.ForgottenBooks.com

Forgotten Books' App
Available for mobile, tablet & eReader

ISBN 978-1-332-85750-0
PIBN 10242252

This book is a reproduction of an important historical work. Forgotten Books uses state-of-the-art technology to digitally reconstruct the work, preserving the original format whilst repairing imperfections present in the aged copy. In rare cases, an imperfection in the original, such as a blemish or missing page, may be replicated in our edition. We do, however, repair the vast majority of imperfections successfully; any imperfections that remain are intentionally left to preserve the state of such historical works.

Forgotten Books is a registered trademark of FB &c Ltd.
Copyright © 2015 FB &c Ltd.
FB &c Ltd, Dalton House, 60 Windsor Avenue, London, SW19 2RR.
Company number 08720141. Registered in England and Wales.

For support please visit www.forgottenbooks.com

1 MONTH OF FREE READING

at

www.ForgottenBooks.com

By purchasing this book you are eligible for one month membership to ForgottenBooks.com, giving you unlimited access to our entire collection of over 700,000 titles via our web site and mobile apps.

To claim your free month visit:
www.forgottenbooks.com/free242252

* Offer is valid for 45 days from date of purchase. Terms and conditions apply.

English
Français
Deutsche
Italiano
Español
Português

www.forgottenbooks.com

Mythology Photography **Fiction** Fishing Christianity **Art** Cooking Essays Buddhism Freemasonry Medicine **Biology** Music **Ancient Egypt** Evolution Carpentry Physics Dance Geology **Mathematics** Fitness Shakespeare **Folklore** Yoga Marketing **Confidence** Immortality Biographies Poetry **Psychology** Witchcraft Electronics Chemistry History **Law** Accounting **Philosophy** Anthropology Alchemy Drama Quantum Mechanics Atheism Sexual Health **Ancient History** **Entrepreneurship** Languages Sport Paleontology Needlework Islam **Metaphysics** Investment Archaeology Parenting Statistics Criminology **Motivational**

THE LIGHT AND TRUTH
OF
SLAVERY.

Reader, here is a picture of the poor, way-faring, degraded Aaron.

AARON'S HISTORY.

There is clear evidence in the life and history of Aaron, that he has been a slave. Aaron cannot read. There are very few full blooded blacks at the South that can read a word, Aaron says.

'Now reader, Aaron wants you to buy this book. I don't want you to buy it merely to read it through, I want you to buy it and I want you to read it, not to lay it up in your head, but to lay it up in your heart, and then you will remember the poor way-faring Bondman. Two thirds of this book was made up by the poor way-faring degraded Aaron. The Bible says, faith without works is a dead article.

Aaron has a great knowledge of the Bible, but cannot read a word.

One mouth and one back to two hands is the law
  That the hands of his Maker has stamped upon man,
But slavery lays on God's image her paw,
  And fixes him out on a different plan:
Two mouths and two backs to two hands she creates,
  And the consequence is as she might have expected,
Let the hands do the best upon all her estates,
  The mouths go half fed and the backs half protected.

"Whose eyes stand out with fatness having more than heart could wish," who will turn a deaf ear to their own flesh when it passes along, and do walk like Priests and Levites clear, and no relief provide. God in his anger down on you looks. A dreadful damning sin. The men that go to Congress, are men of good talents and principles, yet all the horrors and butcheries of slavery they sanction. Aaron thinks they are as destitute of moral principles as a horse.

Now God Almighty has spared us to see almost another new year through a great deal of sorrow and tribulation; but yet he has spared our unworthy bodies so far, and has not sunk us as Mr. Miller has prophesied, but we ought not to make our boast about it, for it may not be too late yet, because we do not know when the Lord will break out in judgment against us, when we are living in so much sin and iniquity, when dangers stand thick through all the land to push us to the tomb, and we would go to the bottom if it were not for a merciful God. He is slow to anger and abundant in mercy. He commands us to touch not and handle not unclean things, but come out from among the wicked and dwell among the righteous. Do we do this? Aaron thinks not. In our free and independent country, where God's holy word is scattered throughout the United States, there is almost three million slaves, and about one million of them the white brethren's sons and daughters. Well you will all unite and uphold the mother of abomination. Now, men, you call yourselves christians, be wise and consistent, and do not go to the polls and vote for a man that will turn you right out of doors. Now when you white friends was running Mr. Harrison for President, they made such a fuss that Aaron thought Mr. Harrison was going to make milk & honey flow through the face of the earth, which when he took his seat he did not live but a short time. God Almighty thundered from the eternal heavens and sent for him, and Aaron trusts he has gone right home to heaven, and Aaron prays God that he may keep him low in the valley of humility, that at the end of the warfare I may have grace to leap right home to heaven, and I trust to hail Mr. Harrison there.

When Tyler came upon the throne, what did he do but turn men right out of office, who had half a dozen little children crying for bread. Now what more can you expect from a slave-holding man, for you can expect nothing more, and if you men would be consistent with your prayers, and pray from the center of your heart, then God would hear and answer and bless your prayers, and let the oppressed go free; but you see you don't pray in faith, believing, that is the reason you cannot see to vote for good honorable men. Their heads are full of knowledge of the Almighty and their hearts are shut up with sin and iniquity. Aaron's views on slavery connected with politics.

AARON'S TRAVELS.

When Aaron struck into New Jersey, it began to grow dark, about two miles before I come to Elizabethtown, it was very cold; I traveled through a swamp about one quarter of a mile.

When I got into Elizabethtown, I was covered with mud up to my knees and almost froze. I fell into several houses and asked them if they would be good enough to let me warm me, but none of them would be good enough. I almost sunk in despair and I thought I would freeze. I fell into a house where there was an old gentleman, and I asked him if he would be good enough to let me come and warm myself, he told me yes, he would; my heart leaped for joy, because I was almost chilled through. Aaron says he had two daughters and they were very fine women, and one of them had lived in Missouri for four years, her husband died and she became a widow. It was a very cold and windy night, and I asked him if he would be good enough to let me lay down in the kitchen all night by the fire. No you shant lay in the house, he said, but you may go and lay in the barn. And his daughter that had become a widow in Missouri, she kept house for her father, she gave Aaron a first rate of a supper, and a pair of dry trowsers to put on, and a good pair of dry socks to put on, and two blankets and a quilt, and she slipped them to me out of the kitchen window; she told me in the morning when I got up to fetch them down out of the hay loft and put them in the carriage. I did so. I came to the kitchen and she refreshed me with a first rate of a breakfast, and I had a long talk with her; she told me after her husband died she went about twelve miles out of the city of St. Louis, and kept school for a planter that owned one hundred and six slaves. She told me he cut up with his female slaves more than he did with his wife; she said sometimes his poor wife was almost crazy, and he tried to cut up the same capers with me, but he missed of it, and he pretended to be a member of the church too. She told me that when the sinful capers was found out by every one of the free States, she thought then slavery would be abolished and not before. She told me she came home to her father's house as quick as she could get away. What a blessed thing it is for any one when they meet with sorrow and afflictions, to have a father's home to go to. Now the poor slave when he is tied up to the whipping post and whipped almost to death, he has no father to protect him, and no mother to protect him, and no one to fly to but his Heavenly Father. They have to bear patiently with their hard task masters, and live humble and faithful to God, and then at the end of the warfare God will richly crown them in heaven.

When I was traveling in Foxboro', I fell in among Universalists, and they entertained the way-faring and degraded Aaron very hospitably, and treated him like a brother, minister and all. They wrote considerable for Aaron towards printing in my book, and throwed in and helped me to some money towards getting it printed. I staid seven days with them. And I bid 'em good bye, and wished the blessing of God upon 'em. Aaron says he wonders there arn't a thousand Universalists to where there is one. He wonders there arn't a thousand infidels in the world to where there is one, because the white brethren believe in the true light and gospel, and sentiments of the Holy Ghost, and yet set a bad example for their white brethren to stumble over. That is what makes me say it is a wonder there is not a thousand infidels and Universalists to where there is one. Men, again, who live up to the moral law, wont enslave their brethren. Aaron says that no true hearted christian will hold his brother in bonds. The bible says, he that stealeth a man and selleth him, shall surely be put to death. If he is found in his hands, that thief shall die. If a man hateth his brother whom he has already seen, how can he love God whom he has not seen. God says, in the eyes of man, there is respect to persons, but in his eyes, there is no respect to persons. Whenever a man is cleansed from his sin and iniquity, he is a new formed creature in Christ Jesus. Christ is in that white friend the hope of glory, and he is in Christ, and so therefore there is no respect to persons. He will treat an African brother as well as a white brother. He will not oppress him. If he is a wolf clothed in sheep's clothing, he will stand up and say it is right to enslave the African brother. But, if he is a sincere, godly man, he will not stand up and say it is right.

When Aaron was in the middle of the town in Wrentham, I fell among several anti-slavery families, and they treated me very coldly, much as ever I could do to get a place to sleep, but the Lord opened the heart of a white brother who had not been living in the place more than six months, who gave me a first rate bed to sleep in, and first rate food to eat. The next morning was a very pleasant one, and I told him if I never saw him no more, that I might have grace to meet him in heaven, and bid him and his family good by.

I fell in with a young minister. * * * * His wife entertained Aaron very hospitably, she asked me if I would not have something to eat, and I thanked her and told her no, but I told her I would take a bite along with me, and, say she, very well ; and so she gave me two or three crusts of bread and a couple of slices of mouldy meet which smelt. And the minister is a very holy man, and he chastised Aaron a couple of times about speaking the Lord's name in vain, but Aaron is afraid he is a wolf clothed in sheep's clothing. With all his holiness, the crust of bread and a couple slices of mouldy meat was good enough for me. I trust that he may get to heaven; and I may be shut out, but He has got to shake off some of the sin connected with his holiness before he will see his father's face in heaven.

Beggars ought not to be choosers, but Aaron did not go in there begging for victuals to eat. I went in there begging them to write a little for me, being as I could not write a word myself, and it is there they did write a little for me. Being as his wife asked me to eat some, I thought she might give me food good to eat, not give me food no better than for a hog to eat, and as poor and in poverty as I am, I never would ask them to eat unless I gave them as good food as I eat. We all ought to learn to be consistent with our holy grace, for Aaron firmly believes that God is a Being that will not be mocked ; he is long-suffering and abundant in mercy, and he that endures unto the end, he richly will crown in heaven, but the hypocrite he will turn a deaf ear to, and shut them out of his holy presence. Aaron thinks if he ever gets to heaven, he will hail a great many Universalists there—them that believe in the true light and gospel of God's holy word. I am afraid a great many of them will have to take a leap in the dark.

Twelve miles before Aaron struck into Uxbridge, I fell in with a Universalist. Aaron did not learn his name, he treated me as a brother, but I never shall forget his form, he did'nt and sorrowful did he promise to pity and shift Aaron for money from friend to friend. He helped him to lodging and to victuals and in money. He told of a quaker man who was a great abolitionist, he lived in Uxbridge. Aaron went to him and he took my letter and read it, and then told me to go about my business. Aaron says it did not astonish me ; the Quaker brethren is like one half of the Methodist brethren, they are complete wolves clothed in sheep's clothing.

When Aaron was in Mendon, the friendly people throwed in and helped me considerable towards getting my book printed. When Aaron was in Blackstone, there was a white gentleman asked me if I had saw ———— ———— brother-in-law, who had lately removed from Connecticut State, and I told him that I had saw his wife, but I had not seen her husband, yet he told me that he pretended to be a great anti-slavery man, and he told me that when I saw him, that he guessed he would give me twenty-five cents.—I went to his house Sunday morning about eleven o'clock, and I told him I had got victuals enough to board myself, I asked him if be would be clever enough to keep Aaron there all night till Monday morning, he told me no, and he would'nt do it, and found as much fault with Aaron as if I had been boarding with him six months. Aaron thinks that instead of being an anti-slavery man that he is a great rebel as ever trod the soil of New England country. Aaron thinks if he had him in the South and he thought he could make one dollar on me, that he would sell me as quick as lightning.

Aaron was born in the South. Aaron's parents have been dead this something like 23 years. Aaron says it was nothing but hard work and hard usage that killed them. That gentleman in Millville, told me there was plenty of work to be done there. There were several told me there were two or three gentlemen in business there that were now broken up, and there was as many as eight or nine men there told me business was very hard.

When a man's heart is shut up with sin and iniquity he generally always speaks what comes uppermost, let it be a lie or the truth, but the lie generally always comes first.

SLAVERY A SIN

We believe slavery to be a sin—always, every where, and only sin. Sin in itself, apart from the occasional rigors incidental to its administration, and from all those perils, liabilities, and positive inflictions to which its victims are exposed. Sin is the nature of the act which created it, and in the elements which constituted it. Sin, because it converts persons into things; men into property; God's image into merchandize. Because it forbids men from using themselves for the advancement of their own well being, and turn them into mere instruments to be used by others solely for the benefit of the users. Because it constitutes one man the owner of the body, soul, and spirit of other men; gives him power and permission to make his own pecuniary profit, the great end of their being, thus strikes them out of existence as beings, possessing rights and susceptibilities of happiness, and forcing them to exist merely as appendages to his own existence, in other words, because slavery holds and uses men as mere means for which to accomplish ends, of which end, their own interests are not a part. Thus annihilating the sacred distinction between a person and a thing; a distinction proclaimed an axiom of all human consciousness; a distinction created by God—crowned with glory and honor in the attributes, intelligence, morality, accountability and immortality, existence, and commended to the homage of universal mind, by the concurrent testimony of nature, providence, conscience and revelation, by the blood of the atonement, and the sanction of eternity, authenticated by the seal of Deity, and in its own nature, effaceless and immutable. This distinction slavery contemns, disannuls, and tramples under foot. This is its fundamental element—its vital constituent principle, that which makes it a sin in itself under whatever modification existing, all the incidental effects of the system flow spontaneously from its fountain head. The constant exposure of the slaves to outrage and the actual inflictions which they experience in innumerable forms, all resulting legitimately from this principle, assumed in the theory and embodied in the practice of slave-holding.

Ah me, what wish can prosper, or what prayer,
For merchants rich in cargoes of despair?
Who drive a loathsome traffic, gauge and span,
And buy the muscles and the bones of man.

Like Mary have you come early to the sepulchre seeking Jesus in the Tomb? Aaron thinks that hundreds and thousands of poor creatures, black and white, die in that manner every year: we never think to call upon our heavenly Father, only when afflictions fall at our heels, then we'll call on our heavenly Father. God commands us to shoulder our cross, to follow him through evil report as well as good. There are a great many live humble and faithful to God, till sorrows and afflictions come against them, then they will flee like deadly poisoned, something like Judas and Peter, they will deny that they ever knew God. Let us all learn to be consistent, not to deceive our brethren, when we have the true love of God stamped in our unworthy hearts, then we'll shoulder our cross and follow Christ through evil report as well as good. Aaron has seen a good many men and women in his travels, the outward appearance appeared to Aaron to be Angels, when Aaron stopped with them a while, and come to have dealings with them, their hearts were as destitute of the love of God as a pitcher,—complete wolves clothed in sheep's clothing.

Now reader, I want you to remember the Bible says he that is thought much of in the eyes of men is despised in my eyes, blessed is he who is despitefully used for my sake; the Bible says that he who calls his brother a fool is in danger of hell-fire. Aaron says that a true witness of Christ is persecuted on the right hand and on the left; are brought as sheep before the slaughter.

When Aaron was in Milford, two angels entertained him very hospitably, made him welcome to stay over the Sabbath, with them; merely stopped awhile to ask their wives to write a little, and they insisted on my staying over the Sabbath day, and Aaron staid with them until Monday morning. I was in the house about fifteen hours, they began to find as much fault with me as if I had begged them to keep me a week. How wrong Aaron thinks it is when a man will stand up and tell his brother one thing, and have his heart another way; a hollow heart is tenfold worse than an Arab, an open enemy is less to be feared than a false friend. These two angels that entertained Aaron on the Sabbath day, were men who professed to be filled with gospel grace, but like Adna and Anthony filled with filthy lucre.

A short sentence from the little book of Bro. Offley's who had a hard fight with the devil. By the help of God he won the great battle, and is now fighting his way onwards towards Heaven.

GENESIS ix. 25.
And he said, Cursed be Canaan; a servant of servants shall he be unto his brethren.

MY DESIRE AND EFFORTS FOR EDUCATION.

I was born in the state of Maryland, at Centreville, in Queen Ann County. I was nineteen years and eight months old, when I had a desire to read the Bible. The free people of color were not allowed to go to school where I was brought up. There was an old colored man living with us who could read, and he told me if I would get a book he would learn me. I bought a book, and I learnt my letters in one day, so that I could say them all perfectly. After the dear old father in the Lord left our house, I was without a teacher.

I went to work for one Mr. Davis; I learnt him the art of wrestling and boxing, and he learnt me to read. But when I got through working there, I always carried my book in my hat, and whenever I met with a white boy any where, I would ask him to learn me a lesson. Sometimes they would, and at other times they would not. I was at a village and I got a little white boy to give me a lesson; the white people talked of mobbing me; they said if I were to learn to read, that I soon would learn to write, and that I would be writing free passes to get the slaves away. I told them that I only wanted to learn to read the Bible. I lived at St. George's, Delaware, two years; there was a family of white people that lived in the village. They had two children; the boy was a very good scholar, and he told me that his father gambled and drank to such a degree that when he came from his work, he had not so much money as would buy them bread to eat, and if I would give him and his little sister something to eat occasionally, that he would come every other night and learn me to write and cypher. The old lady whom I lived with was willing that I should give them what they wanted to eat, and I often took them in the kitchen and gave them something to eat; so he was very attentive, and soon learned me to write and cypher. Sometimes he would stay with me till one, two and three o'clock in the morning. Many has been the night that I have spent, after working all day long, so that I might know when I work for man, whether I receive my just dues. My father is an unlearned man, and has lost many a cent by not knowing how to count.

MY FIRST CONVICTION, &c.

I was convicted of my sins, when I was about eighteen years old. I used to go in the woods and pray three or four times a day. One day a young man heard me; he told my father that he heard some one in the woods praying, though no one knew it was me.

An old backslider told me if I got religion I should not keep it. I was told that the worst place in hell was for a backslider. One white man told me that if a person had religion he would be good for nothing. Why, if a man strikes you on the right cheek turn to him the other also. I thought I would wait till I got to be an old man, and then no one would want to hurt an old man, so I lost all of my conviction and sought to be a bully. I spent one year in learning the art of wrestling and learning to fight. I was taken sick and the devil was after me; I called for my father to come and pray for me, and the devil left me. My second conviction was on account of the death of my sister and two brothers. My sister and youngest brother both died in triumph in the Lord, but my eldest brother, who died on the third day of September, A. D. 1834, while in his illness, said to Mrs. R. Johnson, you must not think hard of me when I make a noise, I am praying and trying to make my peace with the Lord. I promised the Lord that I would pray to him, and seek him from that time forward, and did seek him, but I did not find him; I was making money too fast. I went thirty-five miles to find my sister, Ellen Warner, and my brother Alexander Offley. I expected if I got with them, that I should be converted, but when I arrived there I took too much of the devil's goodness about me. The next year, twelve months from the day my brother died, I was taken sick with the same kind of fever. I thought I should die, and if so I must at once be plunged into hell, but I prayed mightily to God; then all my former sins came in my mind, but I soon got well again, and that conviction partly left me. After a few months, I met with my sister Ellen Warner; she and others offered up prayers for me, and she said if I died and went to hell, her prayers would follow me there. I never got over that prayer, and I was brought to the point of the sword of the Spirit, in my heart. I came to this State, viz. Connecticut, on the 15th of Nov. 1825, and the Friday following I was invited to a meeting. I supposed it was preaching that I was going to, but when I got there, I found it was a class meeting; it was a very dark night, and I did not know the way home, else I certainly should have left before the leader got up to ask me any questions, but I stayed and told them that I was a poor sinner, doomed to death.—I freely would have given the world had it been in my power, rather than been caught in that class meeting.

November 21st, 1835, I went to church in Wapping, East Windsor, and heard brother Chapin preach. After preaching, there was a class meeting, and I took up my hat to go home, but I had not the power to do it. It came to me that this was the day of salvation; all the promises that I had made were before me; then I promised that I never would give over the struggle until I had found a grave for my sins. I went home and went into the barn and kneeled down by the manger, and asked the Lord to have mercy on me a sinner; but I did not feel any better. I gave myself to reading the Bible and prayer. I made it my duty to go in secret and pray from three to seven and ten times a day; as soon as I began to leave off my evil habits, and give myself up wholly to the Lord, I was troubled for about two months and a half, for the devil followed me. Sometimes he would be after me so that I could see him in night visions; sometimes he would be after me in the shape of a large dog; at other times, like a large black bull, and the only way that I got relieved would be by something like a white person. Oftentimes I would be traveling, apparently, with persons whom I knew to be professors of religion, and those dogs and bulls would be ready to devour me, and never notice the Christian people; that gave me to understand that the Christians were on the Lord's side. I was notified that I was on the road to hell, and it was sin that got me there, and nothing but prayer and faith in Christ would put me on the road to heaven. I fasted and prayed every Friday, until noon, from the time I began to seek the Lord until I found him, being three months.

MY EXPERIENCE, FEBRUARY 21, 1836.

On the Lord's day I had been much engaged in prayer and telling to the world my determinations to seek heaven, and the means of grace that I had used. About three o'clock in the morning, I was asleep, and heard a voice call me three times, and the third time I saw a large bird, its wings were the color of a mourning dove, and the downy feathers were white as snow, and it took me by the hand; then I awoke and the room was light as noon day, and I leaped out of my bed and gave God the glory that my sins were forgiven. It was a blessed day and week to my soul. I knew nothing about hatred then. I was like Peter, (Acts x. 10, 11,) and I saw heaven opened and a certain vessel descending unto him, as it were a great sheet knit at the four corners, and let down to the earth.

Then Peter opened his mouth and said of a truth I perceive that God is no respecter of persons. Acts x. 34. But in every nation he that feareth him, and worketh righteousness, is accepted with him. Acts x. 35. One week before my conversion, before the heavenly bird, I was in a vision, and I saw three stars fall from heaven, and they burned up all the wicked, and every thing that stood, except me and the Christians. This gave me new courage and strong faith to trust in the Lord.

MY CALL TO THE MINISTRY.

About three months after I had experienced religion, I heard a voice say to me, go preach my gospel, and I made up my mind to go; and nights, when I was asleep, it appeared that I could hear and see hundreds of people around me, in prayer to God, and sinners getting converted by scores. I often woke myself up singing and praying; some nights I heard such glorious music round my bed, that I was afraid, and the devil told me that if I lived so faithful, I should go crazy, and be of no use to any one, or I should die. Then I began to look at other poor preachers, and thought how they were persecuted; and of the duty that was incumbent on them. My own ignorance was such that I gave up the idea, and as soon as I gave it up, I was again troubled with dogs and various kinds of beasts. I would work sometimes till I was almost exhausted; my mind was so troubled that I did not know, a great many times, what I was about. One of the white ministers told me that I had better go to school, but I thought if the Lord had called me to preach, he could make me just what he would have me, without going to school; so I did not go, and I grieved away the spirit. I looked at the colored brethren, and I beheld thousands of them in slavery, and I turned my thoughts to what I had seen, and I beheld a Christian community who were buyers and sellers of my brethren, and yet they say that they are going to Heaven; here I reasoned with the devil till he out-reasoned me. I looked again and I saw the state of my colored friends, and they were nearly all poor, and I thought of what a slaveholder said to me, if a Negro gets religion he will spend all his time in prayer, and you can never get any work out of him, nights nor Sundays, for he has got to pray all night, and preach all Sundays. The devil told me if I went to preach, I should always be poor, and if I was sick no one would like to trust me, because people would know that if I should die, they would never get any thing.

Southern Arguments to stop the Mouths of Northern Guests.

A Northern man goes to the South, sits at a table loaded from the slaves' unpaid toil, who eats his corn bread in the sun, marries a slave holder, and then finds out that slavery is a divine institution, and defends it in Southern and Northern pulpits, religious newspapers,—and for example consult memory or observation.

Rev. Basil Manly, a clerical man-seller, recently preached in our churches in various parts of N. England, and the scores of clerical Baptist slave-holders that beset the North every summer, are invited to occupy your pulpits. If you would enjoy the smiles of him who came to preach deliverance to the captives, renounce all fellowship with the unfruitful works of slavery, that you may in word and deed reprove them.

A poor slave being on his death bed, begged of his master to give him his liberty before he died. "I want to die free massa." His master replied, you are going to die soon, what good would your liberty do? "O master, I want to die free." He said to the slave, "You are free." "But do write it master, I want to see it on paper." At his earnest request he wrote that he was free. The slave took it in his trembling hand, looked at it with a smile, and exclaimed, "O, how beautiful! O, how beautiful," and soon fell asleep in the arms of death.

TOUSSAINT L'OUVERT.

The friends of the enslaved are continually told that Africans are an inferior race. If this were true it would be no good reason for enslaving them. But it is not. The world may be safely challenged to produce a nobler character than that of Toussaint, the George Washington of St. Domingo. Calumny has striven to paint him a monster. She has brought the printing presses of both continents to her aid, but in vain. Toussaint was born in slavery, but his soul cannot be bound. When his countrymen who had gained their liberty by the proclamation of Santhonax and Polvorre were in danger of losing it by the intrigues of former tyrants, he was selected as their chief. With reluctance he left the bosom of his family to which he was tenderly attached. He gave union and a wise constitution to his countrymen. By his bravery he repelled every foe. Bonaparte it seems obtained possession of the sons of Toussaint, and included them in the splendid bribe which he sent to buy the negro chief, hoping by that detestable policy to make an easy conquest. He was mistaken. Toussaint met his boys with the heart of a father, but immediately sent them back with a letter to Bonaparte, the spirit of which will be shown by the following extracts :

CITIZEN CONSUL :

Your letter of the 27th Brumaire has been transmitted to me by Citizen Le Clerc, your brother-in-law, whom you have appointed Captain General of this Island, a title not recognized by the constitution of St. Domingo. The same message has restored two innocent children to the fond embraces of a doting father. What a noble instance of European humanity ! But dear as those pledges are to me, and painful as our separation is, I will owe no obligations to my enemies, and I therefore return them to the custody of their jailors. You ask me, do I desire consideration, honors and fortune ? Most certainly I do, but not of thy giving : My consideration is placed in the respect of my countrymen; my honors in their attachment ; my fortune in their disinterested fidelity. Has this mean idea of personal aggrandizement been held out in hope that I would be induced thereby to betray the cause I have undertaken ? You should learn not to estimate the moral principle in other men by your own. If the person who claims a right to that throne on which you are seated were to call on you to descend from it, what would be your answer? The power I possess has been as legitimately acquired as your own, and naught but the decided voice of the people of St. Domingo shall compel me to relinquish it. It is not cemented by blood, nor maintained by artifices of European policy. The ferocious men whose persecutions I have put stop to, have confessed my clemency, and I have pardoned the wretch whose dagger has been aimed at my life. If I have removed from this Island certain turbulent spirits, who strove to feed the flames of civil war, their guilt has been first established before a competent tribunal and finally confessed by themselves. Is there one of them who can say he has been condemned unheard or untried ? And yet these monsters are to be brought back once more, and aided by the bloodhounds of Cuba are to be uncoupled and allowed to hunt us down and devour us ; and this by men who dare to call themselves *Christians.*

Seven years previous to this Toussaint sent his sons, then seven and nine years of age, to Paris for education. They were put under the care of a tutor named Coisnou. Bonaparte used this man as a tool to prepare the boys for his purpose. The tutor and his charge having been sent out with LeClerc, Coisnou wrote from Cape Francois to Toussaint who was then at his country seat at Ennery, saying, " The first Consul sends by me your two sons and certain important despatches. Your sons will be with you to-morrow, provided you will give me your word that in case of your not complying with the wishes of the First Consul, they shall be safely returned to the Cape." Toussaint gave his word, and on the morrow, the boys accompanied by Coisnou, were with their fond parents. Toussaint had now the choice of three things. He might break his word and keep his sons; he might comply with the wishes of Bonaparte and keep them, or he might send them back. 'He would neither break his word nor sell his country, and therefore he chose to send them back. It was a proverb in St. Domingo that Toussaint never broke his word.

When Aaron was traveling through Rhode Island State with George Benson, a brother-in-law of Mr. Garrison, I put up at a tavern in Providence, on Criston Hill, a very respectable looking tavern. The tavern keeper, was a man with light hair and light skin, and dressed up in first rate cloth. When Aaron fell in with him I gave him my purse to take care of for me till morning, with forty-eight dollars and seventy-five cents. Out of the 48 75 he gave me the purse in the morning with 25 dollars in it. Besides I paid him twenty-five cents for one naked night's lodging. And Aaron thinks that his heart is more homlier with sin and iniquity than Aaron's face is, else he wouldn't stole that money away from me wilfully. Aaron has seen in his travels them that would sooner rob from me than to help me to any. And any one that will rob from Aaron will rob from the dead on the highway. If they see a dead man lying in the wilderness with a thousand dollars in his pocket, they will go and rob every cent away from him, and then will go and say that he had not one copper in his pocket, and will apply to the town to take him and bury him, and the town will throw in their little mites and bury him after having so much money. Aaron has been much better off all through Maine. And Aaron has been in four towns where they have established Anti-Slavery Societies.

Aaron in his travels has been entertained, and very hospitably with sincere Christians.

Aaron has talked in the Baptist church in the city of Portland to between seven and eight hundred people. Aaron staid among the friendly people five days, and during that time there was about fifty ladies and gentlemen told Aaron they would petition to Congress to pay taxes for the valuable negroes which they vote for every three head, and sold them for fourteen or fifteen hundred dollars apiece, such valuable property, and yet don't pay one cent of tax. When Aaron was in Dedham I fell in with a great anti-slavery man. He keeps a store in Boston. I did not learn his name. He told me he wanted me a couple of days to dig potatoes for him. I asked him what he would be willing to pay me for digging potatoes for him, and he told me 50 cents. I told him I would be willing to work for 38 cents if he would be willing to give me a place to sleep in the house, and he told me he could not let me sleep in the house. I asked him if he could not give me a pallet in the kitchen, and he told me he could not, but says he I will fix you a place in the barn. He lived in a large house. Aaron thinks he had room enough to give me a comfortable bed in the house, but the trouble of it was he had not room enough in his heart to give me a place to sleep in his house. Aaron thinks he is like a great many anti-slavery men. What anti-slavery he has got is lodged in the fore part of the skull, his heart is as empty and destitute of anti-slavery as a pitcher is. With all his great abolition he had not abolition enough to keep me in his house. Aaron says he was good enough to do his work for him. With all his anti-slavery, Aaron says he is not one foot better than the Slaveholder in the South. Aaron's master was a very profane man, and he has called me a damn'd rebel since I have been away, and all the scoundrels he could think of. Aaron says he shall not call me a damn fool, not to my head

"Christians, remember those in bonds as though you were bound with them."

Aaron is acquainted with ministers at the South that live in open adultery with colored women. He has known ministers to tie colored men and women in cellars and whip them secretly till their backs were all dripping with blood. Aaron thinks these white friends in the South that pretend to call themselves Christians, their hands and feet are stained with African blood, which I am afraid in judgment the blood of the Africans and their own children's blood that are enslaved, Aaron thinks it will cry so heavy against them in the judgment that it will sink their poor souls right into hell. When Aaron was traveling in Princeton, Mass., he saw an old gentleman, 70 years of age, and he told him he knew he was from the South if he denied it ever so much, and he asked him how he knew. Why he told me he had been all through the South, and he told him he firmly believed it was the prayers of the poor slaves that saved the South from being sunk.

Assist runaway slaves as you would wish to be assisted.

When Aaron was in Norwich, Conn. State, I got to conversing with a yellow man with light hair and blue eyes, and he told me he shipped on board a ship to go to South Carolina at the time of Nathaniel Turner's insurrection in the State of Virginia. They then passed a law that no free man of color should land on the soil of South Carolina. The constables and other officers came down to search the vessel to see if there were any free men of color to take up and put in the Calaboosa. This yellow man that had light hair and blue eyes, he told the constable he was the colored man, and the constable told him he was a d———d Yankee and a liar, and went down into the kitchen and saw a white man that had black hair and black eyes, but he was a full-blooded white man, but he took him and put him in jail and kept him four days until the vessel was ready to sail, and the white man swore he would never go to the South any more, and he is now one of the greatest abolitionists in the state of Connecticut. This fact can be proved by several white men in Norwich.

Happiness of Slaves.

But we are further told that slaves show by their actions that they are happy. They sing, laugh, dance, and make merry. He is a shallow smatterer in human nature, who does not understand this, that mirth is often rather the effort of the mind to throw off trouble than the evidence of happiness. It shows that a man wishes to be happy, and is trying for it, and is oftener the means of use to get it than the proof that it exists; and as to singing, why do prisoners sing in jails?' We have all heard them. Does it prove solitary cells a paradise? Do jail walls, dingy light, and solitude make men so happy that they sing for joy? They sing to make pleasure for themselves, not to give vent to it. Their singing indicates a mind seeking amusement, rather than one contented with what it has—a mind conscious of a want, and striving to satisfy it, rather than one rejoicing in a full supply. In illustration of this we insert a fact from Dr. Channing of Boston.

"I once passed a colored woman at work on a plantation, who was singing apparently with *animation*, and whose general manners would have led me to set her down as the happiest of the gang. I said to her, your work seems pleasant to you. She replied, No, massa. Supposing that she referred to something particularly disagreeable in her immediate occupations, I said to her, tell me then, what part of your work is not pleasant. She answered with emphasis—'No part pleasant. We forced to do it.'"

What has the Church to do with Slavery.

This depends upon the question whether slaveholding is a sin. If it is, the church of Christ have much to do with it. If it is a sin at all, it is a very great sin. It almost shuts out the blessings of the gospel from a sixth part of our people. It sends a corrupting influence over our whole nation. Look at the 2,250,000 immortal beings used as property, as machines for making money. The evil is too mighty to be seen at one glance. Take a single slave —follow him through a life of hard labor without wages; see how the mind, deprived of proper instructions, shrinks and dwindles under the whip and fetter. See how his heart plundered of its holy affections is delivered over to brutality and corruption. Go to the slave auction! see human forms, from infancy to gray hairs, sold under the hammer. See human souls bartered away for cash. See families that God hath joined together, separated, never more to meet in this world. Count, if you can, the groans, fathom the bitter woes, occasioned by these separations. Sum up the thousands of these scenes that take place every year in the great *domestic slave trade*. Go along with the chained drove, from the Potomac to the Mississippi. Then again, glance your eye on the varied shades and features of these unhappy slaves; and see the sure evidence that white masters traffic in the souls and bodies of their own children. Follow out the investigation into its details, and you will begin to learn the greatness of the sin.

But go forward a little further. Follow to the judgment bar of Christ, all the souls that have been trained up in slavery. Before the same bar will stand the American Church. Will not this immense and woful havoc of souls which God created in his own image, and for whom Christ died, be one of the first things to be inquired of by the judge? Will not every individual Christian be asked, "What hast thou done in this matter?"

Now look and see what the church is doing. See how, in its largest denominations, it embraces in its bosom slaveholders of all sorts. How it abstains from reproof. How, in its most solemn assemblies, slaveholders are mingled and sit down together at the table of the same Lord. Christians at the North say they are opposed to slavery. Count the number of ministers whom they have sent to the South, who are now slaveholders. Ask whether these slaveholding preachers are ever kept out of the pulpit when they visit the north. How many ministers preach against slavery either at the south or at the north? Count the number of churches that bear testimony against the sin by excluding slaveholders like other open sinners, from their communion.

Now, can any Christian man in his senses say, after such an examination, that the church is ready to answer to God for American Slavery? No! The first thing the church has to do with slavery is, to repent, and purify itself from the practice of it. The second is to repent of the great sin of attempting to justify slavery from the scriptures. The third is, to repent and show toward the injured victims of slavery, the spirit of *Him* who came to open the prison door, to unbind the captive, and let the oppressed go free.

In 1834, a man who had resided three years in New York, and bore a good character, was taken out of bed at midnight, and with his wife and son, carried back into slavery by his own cousin.

In the same year, a white man of Newburn, N. C., carried his four slave children to New Orleans, by way of New York, having sold his wife, their mother, to a New Orleans trader three years before.

In the same year a man by the name of Phillips was taken up in New York by a " speculator," to whom he had been sold by his father, and carried to Virginia as a slave. Many honorable names might be mentioned in connection with such facts.

Aaron thinks there are a few white people here at the north that are worse than the slaveholders at the south. They tie up the blacks at the south and whip them to death for little or nothing. Aaron never knew them tied up and whipped to death for nothing. When Aaron was traveling in Connecticut State, about two days before he got into Litchfield, he felt like something was pushing him along and was so sensible of it that he laid down his bundle and looked back, but could not see anything, but felt troubled in my mind. I knowed that something was going to take place, but did not know what it was. When Aaron struck into Litchfield village, I went to a tavern and there my sorrow commenced, and there was eight or nine young men came up and felt of my head, and there was a couple of old gentlemen came up and felt of my head, and they told me I was no fool, and that I had a good head. Some of them wanted to know where I was from; some said I was from South Carolina, but Aaron did not tell them where he was from, but told him he would give him an eleven-penny bit if he would give him a place to sleep. The tavern keeper told me that he would, but like Aaron and Anthony, he lit Aaron up stairs to bed, for the sake of a few pieces of silver. Judas betrayed his Heavenly Father.

Just so that rebel tried to sell my sinful body to the doctors, but the Lord took care of Aaron; same way the Lord delivered me out of the jaws of the Arabs, just so he delivered me out of the jaws of that rebel. Aaron was seventy miles away from home, and Aaron never expected to see the face of his wife any more, but the Lord did spare him to see the face of his wife once more.

Slavery! second born of hell,
   Child of sin and twin of death,
Who thy brood of woes can tell,
   Drawing from the kindred breath!
Pride and hate, and lust and crime,
   Dark revenge and cruelty;
Woes that end not even with time,
   Woes that curse eternity.

After I lived five years in Ohio, my master heard of me and sent after me; but the Lord opened the hearts of friendly white men and they helped me away to the North.

When I struck into Vermont State, for one week I could scarcely step a step, cause I had froze my toes and feet; with good shoes and stockings on too. Little after that time I could pull all my toe nails out like rotten meat; and Aaron has not got a natural toe nail on his feet; my toes were all one winter healing up. And when I come to realize what the Lord had brought me through, I am really astonished; he has kept my unworthy body from freezing to death, and starving to death.

I have been abused very bad, but my master has never sent me to the whipping post, but he has tied me up at home and has whipped me most dreadfully; and so he has, and he has debarred me of going to meeting; he has locked me up down cellar and has kept me there for whole days, and has not suffered me to eat or drink a bit of any thing, for nothing else under heaven only for going to meeting and serving my Heavenly Father.

Aaron thinks that men put too much confidence in one another, they do things in the eyes of poor feeble dying men, they love the praise of their poor feeble dying men, better than they do their Heavenly Father's. And now when a man is made pure in Christ, he is pure indeed, and he does not do things in the eyes of men to get the praise of men. Aaron thinks there is nothing that man can make compared with the Almighty. What man makes is like his poor feeble dying body, it may last between sixty and seventy years, and then fades away. But what God makes is pure and holy, and it lasts forever. Behold the sand in the rivers, how pure it is; behold the waters that God creates, for as it flows through the earth, how pure and good it is. What is better when we are almost choked for drink than a pure drink of cold water, it don't make us giddy or it don't make us sick, it only refreshes our unworthy bodies. Behold the stone how everlasting it is; it lasts forever, does brick last forever? Man makes brick of clay, and to the dust of clay it returns again, the same way God made us, unto dust we return again. Aaron's views of poor feeble hollow hearted dying men.

A great many people tell me about this awful bad amalgamation business, and that when friendly people took me in and set down to the table to eat with them, and when their acquaintance come in to see them, and see Aaron sitting up to the table eating with them, it draws a dead damp on them, it is like Adne and Anthony. Aaron thinks if they would only look in the South, where I come from, it will be a complete ballot box for them, they would put their hand right on their mouth and never utter another word about amalgamation, or any thing else. In the South white men wont suffer black men to look at white women, but they will go and force black women, and there aint eh or Anthony said about it. The very old devil has got his own right foot on the slaveholder's own neck, and Aaron thinks the poor slaveholder cannot see sin and folly until he is shut up among the damned in hell forever.

When Aaron falls in with sincere Christian people, they treat me like a brother, but not as a slave, and they let the way-faring Aaron eat when they eat, and don't keep me waiting till they have done eating, and then give me a crust of bread and a piece of old stale meat in the kitchen, the way a great many ministers do in my travels. Aaron says he should as live go to hear the devil preach as to hear some ministers, because they preach one thing and practise another, and don't begin to live up to their doctrine. We should always practise what we preach to others, for a man of words and not of deeds, is like a garden full of weeds. So Aaron says.

From Georgia' Southern mountains,
　Potomac's either strand,
Where Carolina's fountains
　Roll down their golden sand;
From many a lovely river,
　From many a sunny plain,
They call us to deliver
　Their land from error's chain.

Shall we whose souls are lighted
　With wisdom from on high,
Shall we to men benighted,
　The lamp of life deny?
Salvation, O Salvation,
　The joyful sound proclaim,
Till all in every station
　Shall learn Messiah's name.

What though fair freedom's breezes,
　Blow softly o'er our land,
And each one as he pleases,
　May worship with his hand,
And though with lavish kindness
　The Gospel's gifts are strown,
The negro in his blindness,
　Is left to grope alone.

Ye masters tell his story,
　And you ye heralds preach,
And to the slave his glory,
　Let every Christian teach;
Till from our ransomed natures
　The chains of bondage fall,
And Jesus, only Master,
　Shall freely reign o'er all.

Selections from the Bible.

Paul to the Galations.—5 chap. v. 19. Now the works of the flesh are manifest, which are these:—Adultery, fornication, uncleanness, lasciviousness, idolatry, witchcraft, hatred, variance, emulations, wrath, strife, seditions, heresy, &c. But the fruit of the Spirit is love, joy, peace, long-suffering, gentleness, faith, meekness, temperance, against such there is no law. Bear ye one another's burdens, and so fulfil the law of Christ.

Rev. i. 12—15. And I turned to see the voice that spake with me. And being turned, I saw seven golden candlesticks; and in the midst of the seven candlesticks one like unto the Son of Man, clothed with a garment down to the foot, and girt about the paps with a golden girdle. His head and hairs were white like wool, as white as snow; and his eyes were as a flame of fire.

Dan. 7: 9. I beheld till thrones were cast down, and the Ancient of days did sit, whose garments were white as snow, and the hair of his head like the pure wool.

Thou shalt not deliver unto his master the servant that has escaped from his master unto thee. He shall dwell with thee, even among you in that place which he shall choose in one of thy gates. Where it liketh him best; thou shalt not oppress him. Deut. 23: 15, 16.

He that walketh righteously, and speaketh uprightly; he that despiseth the gain of oppression, that shaketh the hand from holding of bribes, that stoppeth his ear from hearing of blood and shutteth his eyes from seeing evil; he shall dwell on high; his place of defence shall be the munition of rocks, bread shall be given him; his water shall be sure. Isaiah 33: 15, 16.

Aaron's views on God's holy word, strictly forbids us holding our brethren in bonds, and here is several chapters against it.

Is it such a fast that I have chosen? A day for a man to afflict his soul? Is it to bow down his head as a bulrush, and to spread sackcloth and ashes under him? Wilt thou call this a fast, and an acceptable day to the Lord?

Is not this the fast that I have chosen? To loose the bands of wickedness, to undo the heavy burdens, and to let the oppressed go free, and that ye break every yoke?

Is it not to deal thy bread to the hungry, and that thou bring the poor that are cast out of thy house? When thou seest the naked, that thou cover him; and that thou hide not thyself from thine own flesh?

Then shall thy light break forth as the morning, and thine health shall spring forth speedily; and thy righteousness shall go before thee; the *glory of the Lord* shall be thy rereward. Isa. 58: 5—8.

[Therefore] all things whatsoever ye would that men should do unto you, do you even so to them; for this is the law and the prophets. Matt. 7: 12.

Woe unto him that buildeth his house by unrighteousness, and his chambers by wrong; that useth his neighbor's service without wages, and giveth him not for his work; that saith, I will build me a wide house, and large chambers, and cutteth him out windows; and it is ceiled with cedar, and painted with vermilion. Shalt thou reign because thou closest thyself in cedar? Did not thy father eat and drink, and do judgment and justice, and then it was well with him? He judged the cause of the poor and needy; then it was well with him: was not this to know me? saith the Lord. But thine eyes and thine heart are not but for thy covetousness, and for to shed innocent blood, and for oppression, and for violence, to do it.

Therefore thus saith the Lord concerning Jehoiakim the son of Josiah king of Judah. They shall not lament for him saying, Ah my brother! or Ah sister! they shall not lament for him, saying, Ah lord! or Ah his glory! Jeremiah 22d chap. 13 to 15.

Go to now, ye rich men, weep and howl for your miseries that shall come upon you. Your riches are corrupted, and your garments are moth-eaten. Your gold and silver is cankered, and the rust of them shall be a witness against you, and shall eat your flesh as it were fire,—ye have heaped treasures together for the last days. Behold the hire of the laborers who have reapt down your fields, which is of you kept back by fraud, crieth. And the cries of them which have reaped are entered into the ears of the Lord of Sabaoth. Ye have lived in pleasure on the earth, and been wanton, ye have nourished your hearts as in a day of slaughter. Ye have condemned and killed the just; and he doth not resist you. Be patient therefore, brethren, unto the coming of the Lord. James 5th chapter, 1st to 7th verses.

When Aaron was in Hallowell in the State of Maine, a gentleman told him that there were 52 strong anti-slavery families lived in H. but he could not get a soul good enough to take him in. He thinks if it had been winter he should have frozen to death, but providentially it was warm weather. He laid himself down upon a harrow, but the little red and black ants troubled him so he was obliged to seek shelter some where else. He tarried the rest of the night in a privy. When he arose he found a beautiful morning: he walked four miles, then asked a gentleman if he would give him some breakfast; he told him he was drunk and foolish, and ought to go to the Asylum. He proceeded to two houses farther and the Lord opened their hearts. They provided him with a good breakfast, which refreshed him much, and they gave him food enough to last him two meals. The man who refused to give me a morsel they told me was a rich man. Aaron thinks he is rich in this world, but is afraid he will be poor and miserable in the world to come. He left God's blessing with them, and proceeded on nine or ten miles, when a gentleman opened his house for a meeting. The hearers were very attentive; they can hear other things as quick as a clap of thunder; their heads are full of the knowledge of the Almighty, but how does the heart stand? as empty and as destitute of the love of God as a pitcher.

Now you do not hear of their sending many missionaries to Africa. The ministers are afraid they cant get any more servants to steal. God's holy word says that he that sells a man shall surely be put to death, and if he is in his hands, that thief shall die. Aaron says that missionaries that are sent to Africa never will prosper, and he believes that ministers sent to Africa are sent for mere sham, and has told thousands so in his travels.

The last time Aaron went into Connecticut State, I went to see Mr. Ludlow about purchasing my freedom, and when I got into the city of New Haven, there I saw a man that called me by my name, and Aaron was scared so that I could hardly speak. A colored brother took me to Mr. Boardman's house; he advised me not to purchase my freedom, that no free man of color could live there.

The first time I went to New Haven, I was conversant with Mr. Ludlow about purchasing my freedom. He told me he would see about it: the next time I went to New Haven he was gone from there; he had moved to Poughkeepsie, New York State, so Aaron has give up purchasing his freedom, and has tried to content himself here in the North. God is merciful to us all, and he bears with us and forbears with us. A great many of the people are halted and blind so with sin and iniquity, they can't see God's goodness, nor his wrath until it sinks them right into hell, and then they will see and cry for mercy, but God does turn everlasting deaf ear to them; they are shut up among the damned forever. Behold his pouring wrath out upon the people in Gaudaloupe, and destroyed from between 15000; so Aaron says. It was about as great a place in the traffic of human souls as under the whole globe. Behold his wrath pouring out upon the people upon the wide ocean, and sinking thousands in the sea, nothing only for their wickedness, so Aaron says. Behold thousands of men in the world getting mad with one another, going into the field and cutting one another off by the thousands, and leaving hundreds of widows throughout the world desolate with little children around them crying for bread to eat. Wicked bad tyrants were sent to rule the government, which did not know their right hand from their left, so Aaron says, has pressed out these poor men into battle, has had them all cut off. It is nothing only the wrath of God for their sinful wicked bad doings, so Aaron says.

A short passage selected by Aaron from God's holy word.

1. Let not your heart be troubled: ye believe in God, believe also in me.
2. In my father's house are many mansions, if it were not so I would have told you. I go to prepare a place for you.
3. And if I go and prepare a place for you, I will come again, and receive you unto myself; that where I am, there ye may be also.
4. And whither I go ye know, and the way ye know.
5. Thomas saith unto him, Lord, we know not whither thou goest, and how can we know the way?
6. Jesus saith unto him, I am the way, and the truth, and the life; no man cometh unto the father but by me.—John 14: 1—6.

United States! Your banner wears / Two emblems—one of fame; / Alas, the other that it bears / Reminds us of your shame. / The white man's liberty in types, / Stands blazoned by your *Stars*; / But what's the meaning of your *stripes* / They mean your *negro's scars*.

Was man ordained the slave of man to toil? / Yoked with the brutes and fettered to the soil? / Weighed in a tyrant's balance with his gold? / NO! Nature stamped us in a heavenly mould, / She bade no wretch his thankless labor urge, / Nor trembling take the pittance and the scourge.

Oh, Hail Columbia! happy land! / The cradle land of liberty! / Where none but negroes brand, / Or feel the lash of slavery. / Then let the glorious anthem peal! / And drown 'Britannia rules the waves,' / Strike up the song that men can feel, / Columbia rules three million slaves!"

When Aaron was in Athol, I fell into a house where were several in the house, and among them was a sea captain about 70 years old. He had been dealing on the African coast. I had a long talk with him, and he told me the blacks were better off in the United States with their masters than they were in Africa. Says he, when the King's daughter dies, they will slay two or three hundred to honor the King. Aaron says it is a wilful and malicious lie. The Bible says, "no drunkard shall inherit the kingdom of God." Also, "cursed is he that puts the cup to his brother's lip." Also, "no murderer shall inherit eternal life." "Cursed is he that imbrues his hands in his brother's blood." They carry liquor into Africa, and that ain't bad enough, so they carry guns and powder there, also shot and balls, and the sword, make them drunk and then compel them to fight. Whichever tribe conquers will bring to the whites those whom they conquer, and they will buy them by giving in exchange ribbons, beads, red shirts, and one foolish thing and another. Aaron asked the above named captain, who he is afraid is going down to hell with a bundle of sin on his back, if he didn't think God would bless the nation ten-fold, if they would carry Bibles and hymn books there, and send missionaries and teach them that there is a holy God above. Aaron thinks that God would bless Africa ten-fold, and England and America would be blessed tenfold too. Some says, "Where is the nation that has been treated as bad as the poor Africans? Who inhabits the south part of Africa?

Something like two hundred miles of Africa is inhabited by the white men. The natives are cut off and driven back. And what ain't driven off are stolen away and brought here to America and the West India Islands. Their children are scattered among the white folks and held in bonds. It's true the Indians are cut off from their country and driven back, but they ain't catched and made slaves of, and the women taken away from them and forced by white men, the way the poor Africans is. *The way-faring Aaron.*

Aaron's views on freedom and on slavery.

Industry, diligence, and proper improvement of time, are important duties of the young. In youth the habits of industry are most easily acquired, and the motives to it are the strongest, both from ambition and from duty, and the prospects which the beginning of life affords. Industry is not only the instrument of improvements, but the foundation of pleasure. Nothing is so opposite to the enjoyment of life as the state of an indolent mind. Those who are strangers to industry may possess but they cannot enjoy, for it is labor alone which gives a relish to pleasure. We should fly from idleness as the certain parent both of guilt and ruin. We should never let it cross our path while young. Obtain industry in youth and it will never lose its hold.

Aaron says our southern brethren were reared up in complete idleness. They have blacks to wait upon them, to feed them, and carry them to bed when they are between 8 and 9 years old. Reared up in complete idleness, then when they are reared up, they go to gambling and cock-fighting. Aaron's old master and mistress owned eight slaves, and among them was three females. They had to take night about and sit up all night to fan their master and mistress, to keep them cool, after working and toiling all day. Aaron says that if your females remember your brother in bonds as though you were bound with them, and will try to do all that is in your power to deliver them from that sinful indolent life, I long to see the day when the white people live at the South as they do at the North; not debar the poor African who has to toil out under the hot boiling sun, and depriving them of every thing that is just and right in the sight of a holy God.

Aaron thinks according to the reading of the Bible, that God foreknew everything. God Almighty saw that Pharaoh was determined to keep the children of Israel in bondage. God taught such a time that they should keep them in bondage and that time was four hundred years and no longer. If it was right for the Egyptians to hold the Israelites in bonds, the Lord would not have brought them out. Did not the Lord say that he would bring out the Israelites, and bring the Egyptians to judgment. God sent Moses and Aaron to deliver them, and they were something like twenty or thirty years about it, and it seemed that Pharaoh was determined to hold the Israelites in bonds, the devil made a complete fool of Pharaoh, so that he was swallowed up in water and woke in hell. Pharaoh, he bound the chains tighter and tighter around the Israelites. The poor wicked slaveholder that is now living upon the face of the earth, does not know his right hand from his left in bringing the chains tighter and tighter upon the poor slave at the south, and Aaron is afraid that they will not hearken to justice until the Lord sinks them in sin and folly in the same way he did the wicked Pharaoh. God had a foreview of the white man holding the African in bonds, according to the reading of the Bible, because he says, you may go and buy of the heathen, and they shall serve you forever; and they shall be inherited to your children forever: that is, if your hearts are wicked and bad enough to do so,—but remember after death God will bring you into judgment. We must take the bible as it reads, and it is a bitter guide against slavery, if it was not a bitter guide against slavery why does it say in so many different places, " thou shalt not hold thy fellow mortal in bondage." The slaveholders can't see to read the bible, because their hearts are shut up with sin and inquity, and is stained with the African's blood. When every man is dipped in the blood of Christ, he is a new creature in Christ Jesus, then he can see to read God's holy word, and he will not read it and say it is right to hold his fellow mortal in servitude, and traffic in his own flesh and blood. Any man blessed with moral principles will not stand up and justify slavery and say that is right. Now we just as well might say, that it was right for God Almighty to send down his holy Son from above for the wicked Jews to put to death. God Almighty sent his holy Son down from above to preach to the people to tell them the way to fly from iniquity and be saved in his holy kingdom, but the Jews were very wicked and bad like the people now-a-days, they took the holy Lamb and slayed him. God Almighty blessed the Jews with the power, and he blessed them with the strength, but he did not bless them in the heart with that wicked bad deed. Who was it blessed them with that wicked bad deed? Aaron thinks it was the devil that blessed them with that wicked bad deed, else they would not have taken that holy lamb from above and put him to death. Aaron thinks all the Jews that condemned Christ is now numbered among the damned in hell and always will be there till the end of time. All the horrors and iniquity of slavery Aaron has seen in the State of Maryland and the State of Kentucky, and in the State of old Virginia. Aaron says they do not raise rice there, they do not raise cotton there, this all grows in South Carolina and Georgia. Aaron says that in the last of December they fetch up sugar and molasses, they fetch up rice and cotton, and trade it off in old Virginia for little black boys and girls, between 6 and 7 years old, and take them down into South Carolina and Georgia, and sell them and get the money for them, and put the money in their pockets. Poor mothers are robbed of their dear little children, and there is not ethram nor anthema said about it. Aaron's views upon half-hearted Christian people, standing up in the eyes of their brethren and sisters, and not only in their eyes but in the eyes of a holy God too, and justifying slavery and saying it is right.

Aaron, how did you feel and fare, for about the first week after you left your master.

O good man, after I and tother slave that come with me took start away from our master, for more than one week, I suffered dreadfully, so I did, cause I all the time did think master's overseers were close my heels behind to catch me, and I like most starved to death, so I did,—for after I got into Ohio State with nothing with me to eat, and you know I was afraid to stop at the houses where folks was, to beg; so afraid some enemy would catch me, you know, and run me back to master; which I dreaded that most like death itself, so I did.

And dear man, how I lived I don't know, for as true as you live, I had to creep when it was dark to get where folks did keep their stuff for the hogs to eat, and did eat the very swill, so I did, not as we read the Prodigal Son did in the Bible, because he left his father's nice home; but because I was going to get that freedom which God blessed me to get; that freedom which you white folks have, and don't think much about it. Your white folks tell a good deal about this nation's liberty the fourth of July.

And folks tell me, when the voters meet to choose the people's rulers to serve their master God in his fear and for the constitution liberties of every body in this big nation; but I guess your white voters don't mean or else don't care much about the poor slave; because if they did, I guess they would not vote to make the President of the nation out of slaveholders or some men just as bad as slaveholders, if they don't hold slaves; for so the folks tell me, and I guess it's true.

When Aaron was traveling in Connecticut State, I stopped at a tavern in Windsor, along the Connecticut River, it was pretty cool weather. I asked the tavern keeper if he would'nt be good enough to give me a comfortable straw bed to sleep in for twenty-five cents. He told Aaron his customers did not like it when he took in a colored man. I then asked him if he would'nt be good enough to give me a pallet in the bar-room, he would not do it, and I had to come away. I went about a quarter of a mile farther, and stopped to a young lady's house. She told me she would willingly take me in, but her husband did not like colored people, and he would only scold me if I took you in. She told Aaron to go to the minister, he was a good benevolent man, and he would give me a good comfortable bed to sleep in. I went as she told me to, and asked him if he would be good enough to give me a place to lie down in his kitchen, and he would not do it. Then I asked him if he would not give me an old blanket, and let me sleep in his barn,—he told me he could not very well. Aaron bid him good night, and told him the Lord would provide somewhere for me to sleep to-night. I went about a quarter of a mile further, and the Lord opened the heart of a white widow lady, and she took Aaron in. I told her if she would give me a place to lie in the kitchen, I would put my hand on my mouth and thank God. I was very tired and weary—she told me I should not sleep in the kitchen. But she gave me a candle and told me what chamber to sleep in, and I went up stairs to bed,—and Prince Edward never slept in a better bed,—and she and her son made me welcome to stay over the Sabbath. With all his Christianity the minister had not grace enough to keep Aaron one night in his barn. Aaron says it did not astonish him, for Aaron thinks that two thirds of the ministers' heads are filled with knowledge of the Almighty, but their hearts are empty and destitute of the love of God, as an empty pitcher. They preach more for money, and popularity, than they do for the people's poor souls. That is the reason why sin and iniquity so much abound in the land. If these ministers were men after God's own heart, slavery would not abound in the world as it does, but when sorrow and affliction comes against them they will flee like lightning, but they cannot preach unless you give them fifteen or sixteen hundred dollars a year, then they will preach,—for preaching free salvation to all mankind. If they were men after God's own heart, they would preach for two or three hundred, and they will not rob the widow, and the halt and the blind.

PIOUS SLAVEHOLDERS,—BY ELIZUR WRIGHT.

"I have no more disposition than I ever had, to demonstrate how much men may dabble with dishonesty, or defile themselves with oppression, and yet be saved—how much men may vocally or silently consent with thieves, and yet be honest—how much they may involve themselves with laws and customs worthy of devils, and yet deserve sympathy and consolation at our hands as Christians. There may be Christian pickpockets, Christian horse thieves, Christian swindlers, for aught I know. I am not profound on this argument. But I think such Christians do no honor to a church; much less to a pulpit."

January 15, 1842, Aaron was traveling through Assonet. I stayed all night at the house of Mr. Nichols, and he entertained me very hospitably. I left his house next day between three and four o'clock, you all know the days are very short and cold here at the north. When I left his house the wind blew very cold and night come upon me, and I thought I should freeze. I asked eight or nine families to entertain me, but I could not get any of them to keep me, and I traveled on, and God opened the heart of a good Samaritan, and she entertained Aaron, and she entertained me like a brother, and her husband was almost three thousand miles away from home, and not a soul was in that house but her and four small children, and yet she was not afraid to entertain the wayfaring Aaron. It was a dreadful keen, cold night, but the Lord watched over all that dwelt under that roof, and brought us all to behold the light of another beautiful morning, and she refreshed my unworthy body with a first rate breakfast,—fried beef steak, and good light biscuit, and she gave me a first rate cup of tea that struck through every nerve, and that was not all she done for Aaron, but she told her oldest son to go out and hitch up the horse, and we got in and she toated me all the way to Fall River, that is five miles she carried me,—and she gave Aaron 25 cents in money. She was one white lady out of a thousand. She took Aaron in and kept me from freezing to death, and she gave me first rate victuals to refresh my unworthy body. Her name I have forgotten, but her face will always be in my presence forever.

She is the daughter of the Rev. Mr. Anderson, of Assonet,—he has been Pastor of the Church in Assonet for 40 years. He was a revolutioner.

Aaron has been a slave at the south, and has seen pretty hard times, and also in the west and in the north. Aaron has been through all the New England States, and has told his sorrow and affliction in thirty-two churches, besides in halls, and school-houses, and dwelling-houses. These sorrows and afflictions can be proved by seventy thousand men, which the poor slave has to undergo in getting away from the hard task-masters. Aaron says, if the white men were all like Ward Richards in West Bridgewater, Jesse Torrey in North Abington, Mr. Foster in New Hampshire State, who was dragged out of the church in Nashua, Orson Murray in Vermont State, who prints the Vermont Telegraph, Mr. Gay in Hubbardston, Mr. Bradford, who preaches in the Congregationalist Church in Hubbardston, William L. Garrison, who was dragged through the streets of Boston with a rope around his neck, Mr. Hanning in Cadus in Ohio State, Mr. Stansbury in Lancaster, Ohio, and Dr. Caleb Swan of Easton, there would not be a slave in the United States; but they are not like these men. Aaron thinks God has got a crown richly laid up in heaven for these men who have suffered heavy persecution on the right hand and on the left, because they have stood up for the rights and liberties of the poor African man, who is good enough to stand up and fight for the country in time of trouble, and who have been slain down by hundreds, but are not good enough to enjoy their freedom under these free and independent colors. These free and independent colors float at the Capitol.—Aaron says, in this free and independent country there are almost three millions of slaves kept.

A lash on the back is valued at 40 cents in Virginia and Illinois. The law which is common to both States, runs thus:—In all cases where free persons are punished by fine, servants shall be punished by whipping, after the rate of twenty lashes for every eight dollars, so that no servant shall receive more than forty lashes at any one time—only 16 dollars worth of whipping at one time!

The Slave Joseph.—Come, said Judah, and let us sell him to the Ishmaelites. And the rest agreed to it. Then there passed by Midianite merchantmen, (slave traders,) and they lifted up Joseph out of the pit, and sold Joseph to the Ishmaelites for twenty pieces of silver, poor boy. His father had sent him on a kind errand to his brothers, and was waiting for him to return.

A Southern gentleman, in a debate at Lane Seminary, thus describes the punishment of the *paddle*:

"A bricklayer, a neighbor of ours, owned a very smart young negro man, who ran away, but was caught. When his master got him home he stripped him naked, tied him up by his hands in plain sight and hearing of the academy and of the public green, so high that his feet could not touch the ground; then tied them together, and put a long board between his legs to keep him steady. After preparing him in this way, he took a paddle, bored it full of holes, and commenced beating him with it. He continued it leisurely all day. At night his flesh was literally pounded to a jelly. It was two weeks before he was able to walk. No one took any notice of it. No one thought any wrong was done."

The following instance occurred near Natchez: (See N. Y. Evangelist for Jan. 31, 1835.)

"A planter purchased a notorious runaway. He gave him to understand that he could elope if he chose, probably in a tone which warned him of the consequences. The negro took him at his word, but he was soon taken and flogged very severely. His master then opened the gate and told him to go again; he did so, but was in a few days retaken. His master flogged him if I recollect, till he fainted, and yoked him in the fence between rails, during the day. The wretched negro escaped a third time, but was able to elude pursuit only for a few days. This time his master beat him till his back was almost raw, knocked out his eye teeth, yoked him in the fence, and poured spirits of turpentine over his bleeding wounds. The poor negro fainted on account of the intensity of his sufferings. My informant received his account from the planter."

The two following cases are communicated by Mr. Birney, of Kentucky:

"Not very long ago, in Lincoln county, Kentucky, a female slave was sold to a southern slaver, under most afflicting circumstances. She had at her breast an infant boy three months old. The slaver did not want the child on any terms. The master sold the mother and retained the child. She was hurried away immediately to the depot at Louisville, to be sent down the river to the southern market. The last news my informant had of her was, that she was lying sick, in the most miserable condition, her breasts having risen inflamed and bursted."

"During the winter, at Nashville, a slaver was driving his train of fellow-beings down to the landing to put them on board a steam boat, bound for New Orleans. A mother among them having an infant about ten months old to carry in her arms could not keep pace with the rest. The slaver waited till she came up to where he was standing; he snatched it from her arms, and handing it over to a person who stood by, made him a present of it. The mother bereft in a single moment of her last comfort, was driven on without delay to the boat. On the side of the oppressor was power, but she had no comforter."

A man, I did not learn his name, in Scott county, Tennessee, kept a room apart which no one entered but himself and slaves. One poor man he kept in it two or three days, going in often and whipping him. No one of the family dared, if they wished, to go to his rescue. His cries and groans were so dreadful, that the third night, a young lady living there, got the key secretly, and went to the room. A most appalling sight presented itself to her view: the floor covered with blood and pieces of flesh! She released the almost murdered man; he fled, and had not been heard from. The shrieks extorted by this cruel man were often heard on neighboring plantations, at midnight, day dawn and other times.

THE BLIND MOTHER.

I saw a mother! in her arms
Her infant child was sleeping,
The mother, while her infant slept,
Her guardian watch is keeping.

Around its little tender form
  Her snow-white arm was flung
And o'er its little infant head
  Her bending tresses hung.

Sleep sweetly on my darling babe,
  My own, my only child,
But as she spoke the infant woke,
  And on its mother smiled.

But oh! no friendly answering smile
  The mother's visage graced,
For she was blind and could not see
  The infant she embraced.

But now he lisped his mother's name,
  And now the mother pressed
Her darling much loved baby boy
  Unto her widowed breast.

But sudden anguish seized her mind,
  Her voice was sweetly wild,
My God, she cried, but grant me sight
  One hour, to see my child.

To look upon its cherub face,
  And see its father's there;
But pardon if the wish be wrong,
  A widow'd mother's prayer.

And as she spoke her anguish grew
  More loud and yet more wild,
And closer to her aching breast
  She clasped her orphan child.

———

We shall be over-run with them.

'If Ghosts were flesh and blood and flew in flocks, the spectres of beggary and crime conjured up by "we shall be over-run by them," would darken all our northern air. This objection when waged against our measures, implies the conviction that they will be successful. When argued against emancipation, it implies that slaves are kept there against their will. It implies also that those who make it would keep their slaves in their chains, rather than run the risk of having here and there a colored neighbor. If the objector were to see the slaveholder knocking off the chains, throwing away the whip, and giving wages to his laborers, he must needs cry out, stop! stop!! if you pay your laborers and treat them well, they will quit you and rush to the north. Who makes this outcry? An American, who, while he boasts that his country is an asylum for the oppressed of all nations, would perpetuate the oppression and robbery of his own countrymen, lest some of them should find an asylum in his own neighborhood. But his objection is a bald prophecy, based on no facts, contradicted by history and human nature. If slavery were abolished the slaves would choose to stay at the south as hired laborers, rather than come to the north. Reason : 1. They are already there, and the trouble, expense, distance to be travelled, time necessary for journey, &c. would forever dissuade the main body from migration to the north.

2. There is far more room for them in the slave-holding portions of the U. S. than in the non-slaveholding. In the former there is one-third more territory and one-third less population than in the latter.

3. The climate of the South is congenial to them, that of the North uncongenial.

4. There is far less prejudice against the colored man there than in the North.

5. They are remarkable for their local attachments. This is one of their peculiarities every where; wherever they are to be found, their aversion to a change of residence, especially to a distant removal, is proverbial. All travelers in Africa unite in this testimony; Edward's History of the West Indies, Walsh's Sketches of Brazil, Matherson's notices of Sumatra, Dr. Dickinson's Mitigation of Slavery, Sturge and Harvey's West Indies in 1837, Thome and Kimball's Six Months in Antigua, Barbadoes and Jamaica, abound with testimony to this trait.

We insert from the latter work, a few testimonies of ex-slaveholders in Antigua :—The negroes are not disposed to leave the estates on which they have lived, unless they are forced away by bad treatment.—H. Armstrong, Esq.

Nothing but bad treatment on the part of the planters, has ever caused the negroes to leave the estates on which they were accustomed to live.—S. Bourne, Esq.

The negroes are remarkably attached to their homes.—James Howell, Esq.

The negroes are peculiar for their attachment to their homes.—S. Barnard, Esq.

Love of home is very remarkable in the negroes. It is a passion with them.—Dr. Daniels, Member of Council.

An aged planter said, " they have very strong local attachments. They love their little hut, and will endure almost any hardship before they will desert that spot ;" and Aaron says, he has formerly been a slave at the south, and is eye-witness to it. Messrs. Thome and Kimball say : " Such are the sentiments of West India planters, expressed in the majority of cases spontaneously, and mostly in illustration of other statements. We did not hear a word that implied an opposite sentiment. One gentleman observed that it was a very common saying with the negroes, ' Me nebber leave my bornin ground :' i. e. birth-place."

The slaves rarely run away from mild masters now. When they become their own masters and are protected by just laws, why should they leave their native region to roam among strangers in an uncongenial clime ?

Slaves when emancipated in the South, stay there unless driven out. Farther he says, " the forces were daily increasing, and they felt themselves so strong and secure that they had commenced several plantations on the fertile banks of the Apalachicola, which would have yielded them every article of sustenance, (can slaves take care of themselves?) and which would consequently in a short time have rendered their establishment quite formidable, and highly injurious to the neighboring States."

Composed by Mrs. Mellen of Foxborough, the Universalist minister's wife.

  Heard ye the wail that was borne on the breeze?
  From the land of the south it was wafted;
  Where cruel oppression reposeth at ease
  And liberty's scions are blasted?

  'Twas the wail of the black man, he longs to be free
  From the scourge of oppression that binds him,
  And he weeps when he thinks of his home o'er the sea,
  And the friends that he left behind him.

  For once he was free in the land of his birth,
  Till the white man o'er the ocean came sailing;
  And tore him away from his home and his hearth,
  While they turned a deaf ear to his wailing.

  They bound him in chains and dragged him away,
  And in a dark dungeon confined him;
  Like a felon deprived of the light of the day,
  With strong iron chains they did bind him.

  They then hoisted their flag—'Twas *the flag of the free!*
  And set sail for their home o'er the billows;
  And talked with delight of the friends they should see
  At home 'neath their own native willows.

  But alas! for the black man no kind friends await,
  Him to greet in the land of the stranger;
  Oppression and slavery must now be his fate,
  And no kind hand will shield him from danger.

  And this in a land where the rich and the poor,
  Proudly boast of their free institutions,
  The scourge of the tyrant he must meekly endure,
  Nor claim for his wrongs restitution.

  America, boast not thy freedom again,
  Till thou hast crushed the foul head of the demon;
  Till slavery no more shall exist but in name,
  And thy banners wave o'er none but freemen.

"Aaron was acquainted with a yellow man that lived in Virginia, in the neighborhood where he lived, and the first wife that this man took belonged to his master, and he lived with her about six years, her master then sold her and two children to a man who was going to Georgia, he then swore that he never would take another woman that belonged to his master; he then took a woman about eleven miles from where he lived, and they had three children. His master whipped him three times for going to see his wife and children, and the last time he whipped him it was the cause of his death,—he lived about a week afterwards, and when his poor wife got the news she became crazy and died with grief in about a month, and left three little children in the hands of the Arabs to be bought and sold, and perhaps whipped to death, as their parents were. Aaron has known several instances beside where slaves have been tied up and whipped to death by their masters. Aaron does not know his age correctly, but supposes he was about 29 or 30 years of age when he left Virginia, and in all his life-time in the State of Virginia, he has never known of but one instance of a slave killing his master. The slave was a man three-fourths white, and his master whipped him severely for gambling, and he took a knife and run his master through the heart, and after he had killed his master, his father-in-law shot the slave down without judge or jury. This circumstance, Aaron says, run through the State of Virginia like lightning; if it had been a white man that killed a black man there would not have been ethron or Anthony said about it; this circumstance took place in Virginia 16 or 17 years ago. When Aaron was in Providence there was a white gentleman took me to a colored woman's house to stay over night, and I had a long talk to her before I went to bed; and she told me she was acquainted with a rich white gentleman who lived in Providence, and she used to go and wash every Tuesday for that family, and he did not enjoy good health, and in the winter season he used to go to the south for his health. The third winter he went he took a colored boy with him to wait upon him. When he came home he did not bring the boy with him, and when asked concerning the boy, he said the boy died at the south. God spared him to see another winter and he went to the south again, and took another colored boy with him, and when he returned in the spring no boy came with him, and when asked what had become of the boy, he said he had died, and that the southern climate did not agree with the northen negroes. A few months afterwards he was taken sick, and the day before he died he called to his attendants to " *take away those colored boys, take away those colored boys,*" and the doctor and his friends thought it was the devil he imagined he saw. About a week after he died, the last colored boy he took to the south with him came home. His parents were astonished and rejoiced to see him, and asked why he did not return with the gentleman he went out with. He said the gentleman sold him. His parents were astonished and indignant that a gentleman in whom they reposed so much confidence, should have been guilty of such an inhuman act, and had he been living, he would have been punished to the full extent of the law. Aaron thinks when the man died he went right to hell, for the Bible says, " He that stealeth a man, and selleth him, shall surely be put to death, if he is found in his hands, that thief shall die."

When Aaron was in Braintree, he talked there in the Baptist meeting house; while in the house, a gentleman came and shook hands with him and said, he was not an abolitionist, but says he, " I pity the poor slave, but one half of the abolitionists are so false I cannot take sides with them;" said he, " I am acquainted with a minister in Braintree who professes to be a warm advocate of antislavery and lectured in many of the neighboring towns on the subject. He went to the south and married a woman who owns 160 human beings. He comes back, and apologises for it, and says slavery is not so bad as he formerly thought it was. He has found out it is a money making business." Aaron thinks he is like Lot and Abraham; when they were traveling together, they fell out about their herds of cattle, and Abraham said I pray thee let there be no strife between my herd and thy herd. Lot lifted up his eyes and discovered all the plains of Sodom and Gomorrah, and it was well watered and well grassed, but the people were wicked before the eyes of man and before the eyes of the Almighty, but Lot cared more for the good things of this world than for the company of gospel people. Abraham was a man shod with gospel grace, he was unmovable in the work of the Almighty and he did not go down there and dwell with those wicked people, but directed his way among the righteous. Our land of the south, like Sodom and Gomorrah, is blessed by nature with all that can add to the comfort of man. But the institution of slavery pollutes the moral and religious character, and those who live in the north who go down to dwell with them, are often corrupted and made partakers in the gain of their unworthy traffic, and all their correct ideas of the right of our fellow beings disappear before the love of the root of all evil.

When Aaron was in Bellingham, I fell in with a white gentleman who appeared to be interested and wanted to have me talk. And said he, come let us go to the house of the Baptist minister. I went with him to the house of the minister and had a talk with him: And Aaron was very degraded in the minister's eyes, with all his Christianity. And the gentleman who accompanied me insisted on my lecturing. He thought L had not sense enough to tell what I had seen all the days of my life concerning slavery. He gave out notice, however, for me to lecture, but took good care to prevent my lecturing in the meeting house; but consented that I should hold forth in the school house. For I should be laughed at and made game of by a parcel of loafers who would gather around. Aaron has lectured in several meeting-houses; among which may be named one in Newburyport and one in New Bedford, and in several other places, to large audiences. Aaron thought if he was not good enough to lecture in the meeting house he would not lecture at all. This clergyman, like a great many others, pretends to remember his brother in bonds as bound with them, when he does not remember his brother in bonds as bound with them. In Aaron's travels he falls among ministers who will entertain him, and entertain him very hospitably, that is if I will stop and attend meeting and hear them preach. And then if I am laughed at and made game of what do they care. But when Aaron asks them to get up a meeting for him, that draws a damper on their feelings. I do not know what they are afraid of, except that degraded as I am, I may throw some light before the people, so that their congregations may be broken up, so that they will not have fifteen or sixteen hundred dollars to put into their pockets yearly on which to live in fine style, while their poor brethren at the south are in the worst of bondage. I Aaron thinks they preach more for money than for the people's poor souls.

' Haste makes waste, and waste makes want.' Let us be certain that we have got the mote out of both our own eyes, and then we can see to pick it out of our brother's eye. Whenever a man is born of God, then he is a new creature in Christ Jesus. Christ has in that white framed a hope of glory, and he is in Christ, and therefore they are as one, God will not bless and convert our souls from sin and iniquity unknown to us. When God blesses and converts our unworthy souls we have the witness abiding within. Now brethren and sisters let us be wise and consistent, let us remember the sin and iniquity that abounds in our land. When our brethren come to us to get assistance for the foreign mission, we will have our eyes open, then we can tell them with a clear conscience of the horrors, and evil, and iniquity that abound in our land.

Behold the horrors, and sin, and iniquity, of slavery.

Whenever all of our hearts are cleansed from sin and iniquity, then we can see the horrors and evils of slavery, and every wicked, bad sin, that abounds in our gospel and christianized country. Aaron's views on the state of things.

Reader, here is a short sentence from poor Nat Turner, who suffered almost everything in the swamps for one year at Northampton; finally he was taken and hung; this took place about fifteen years ago.

Human flesh bought and sold, and chained together rank and file; the mastiff is kept to hunt human souls, and this is all done over God's holy word. We have a great many meetings in the southern countries; what good does it do? We are commanded to watch and pray and keep old Lucifer under our feet; whenever any one is pure in the blood of Christ, they do this. The Christians in the south, instead of keeping Lucifer right under their feet, they let Lucifer have his foot right on their necks, and by and by they'll fall, and great will be their fall, for they will fall to rise no more. This is what the wayfaring Aaron requested me to write for him. When I was in Ohio, about 20 miles from Chillicothe, Aaron and Ben pitched a tent along the Sciota river, and there we remained for four days. Aaron goes and gets a pot that they keep in the barn to grease the wagons, and takes it to my little tent and cleans it, and then goes and gets raw potato parings out of the swill and cooks them. One day Aaron went and got an old shank bone and cooked it. It was a great place for hunting. Aaron went out to gather some chips early in the morning, a hunter came very near shooting Aaron through the head; we were obliged to leave that spot, as it was dangerous for us to tarry there. We did'nt put up quarters any where till we reached Lancaster, the way we went was one hundred miles. After I was in Lancaster 4 years, I got to conversing with Mr. Stansbery; he told Aaron that he had traveled all along the Sciota river, and I told him about my little tent, I had built along the Sciota river, and he told me that he saw the same tent, and Aaron thinks it is there to this day.

Some days after I left my master, I thought I heard some one following me. It was in a woody, swampy piece of land. I turned my shoes hind side before, to make them think I was going the other way, and went about two miles in the swamp, and Aaron thinks the Lord looked down upon me and put wisdom in my unworthy head.

On the 9th of May, 1844, Aaron was traveling through Spencer, in Mass., he fell into the house of ——————, was hungry, tired and weary, and asked Mr. —— for leave to lie down upon his kitchen floor, and understood him yes. He went in and saw his little daughter, whom he asked to lend him a teapot to make himself some tea. Her mother came and looked cross and savage at him, and asked what he wanted. He replied I want to make a little tea. She refused him, and liberty to lie upon the floor, and bid him be off, a black rascal. He went on, but God opened the heart of a good Samaritan, who would not allow him to make use of his own, but gave him of her tea, and gave him a bed to rest his unworthy body, which the other and his wife had not grace enough in their heart to do,

Deut. 15: 1—14. "At the end of every seven years thou shalt make a release. And this is the manner of the release: every creditor that lendeth aught unto his neighbor shall release it; he shall not exact it of his neighbor, or of his brother, because it is called the Lord's release; Of a foreigner thou mayest exact it again, but that which is thine with thy brother, thine hand shall release, save when there shall be no poor among you, for the Lord shall greatly bless thee in the land which the Lord thy God giveth thee for an inheritance to possess it: Only if thou carefully hearken unto the voice of the Lord thy God, to observe to do all these commandments which I commanded thee this day. For the Lord thy God blesseth thee, as he promised thee, and thou shalt lend unto many nations, but thou shalt not borrow; and thou shalt reign over many nations, but they shall not reign over thee. If there be among you a poor man of one of thy brethren within any of thy gates in thy land, which the Lord thy God giveth thee, thou shalt not harden thine heart nor shut thine hand from thy poor brother: But thou shalt open thine hand wide unto him, and shalt surely lend him sufficient for his need in that which he wanteth. Beware that there be not a thought in thy wicked heart, saying, the seventh year, the year of release is at hand; and thine eye be evil against thy poor brother, and thou givest him naught; and he cry unto the Lord against thee, and it be sin unto thee. Thou shalt surely give him, and thine heart shall not be grieved when thou givest unto him; because that for this thing the Lord thy God shall bless thee in all thy works, and in all that thou puttest thine hand unto, for the poor shall never cease out of the land: Therefore I command thee saying, thou shalt open thine hand wide unto thy brother, to thy poor and to thy needy in thy land. And if thy brother, an Hebrew man, or an Hebrew woman, be sold unto thee, and serve thee six years, then in the seventh year thou shalt let him go free from thee. And when thou sendest him out free from thee, thou shalt not let him go away empty; thou shalt furnish him liberally out of thy flock, and out of thy floor, and out of thy winepress; of that wherewith the Lord thy God hath blessed thee thou shalt give unto him."

Shall the United States, which cannot bear the bonds of a king, cradle the bondage which a king is abolishing? Shall a republic be less free than a monarchy? Shall we in the vigor and buoyancy of our manhood, be less energetic in righteousness than a kingdom in its age?—C. Stewart.

Shall every flap of England's flag
Proclaim that all around are free,
From farthest Ind to each blue crag
That beetles o'er the Western Sea,
And shall we scoff at Europe's kings
When freedom's fire is dim with us,
And round our country's altar clings
The damning shade of slavery's curse;

Go let us ask of Constantine,
To loose his grasp on Poland's throat,
And beg the lord of Mahmoud's line
To spare the struggling Suliote,
Will not the scorching answer come
From turban'd Turk and fiery Russ,
Go loose your fettered slaves at home,
Then turn and ask the like of us.

We northern men have to pay taxes for so many head of cattle, and so many head of horses,—and if they own houses, they have to pay taxes for them; and if they own land they have to pay taxes for that. Now our white brethren at the south have to pay taxes for these, houses and lands, and their horses and cattle, so Aaron says. Aaron says for their human cattle they do not pay one cent of tax, and for these human cattle they will sell for eight to fifteen hundred dollars,—so much profit to them,—and yet do not pay taxes for them. Aaron says that there was a gentleman in the town of Lynn told him the town of Lynn had lost one million dollars by the south. Aaron says there was a gentleman in the town of R. told him that the town of R. had lost fifty or sixty thousand dollars, and several other towns that had lost money by the white brethren in the south, (so Aaron says.) At Norfolk there is between two and three hundred soldiers kept there. What are they kept there for? Why to keep the blacks in slavery. Our free and independent colors float there at the capitol; so they do, and Aaron says there is almost three million slaves held in bondage under these floating colors. Now where does the support come from that keeps these soldiers there? Why pretty much the whole heft comes out of the north.

You white friends will all unite together, instead of rising and shaking the dust off your feet and having nothing to do with them bad tarlims in the south; but Aaron is afraid that your white friends will unite together, and will leave you as poor as poverty, as the poor slave is, before you see the horrors and the evils and the iniquity of slavery.

Aaron has traveled through twelve different States, and one hundred miles in Canada, and never was entertained so hospitable in my life as I was by Mr. Ward Richards in West Bridgewater. And if I never see him no more, I pray God I may have grace to meet in heaven. And I was traveling in South Bridgewater, and fell in with a white lady, but I did not learn her name; and I asked her if she would not be good enough to sell me a slice of wheat bread; and because I called her *honey*, she got very angry with me. I did not mean any harm by calling her honey, but she had a great deal of southern temper in her, but she is unconscious of everything that's reasonable. She called Aaron a damned black scoundrel, and all the names she could think of, and hailed to her husband to come way from the lower part of the field; and he came running with a hoe, and leaped over a fence about four foot high, and he hollered, ho ye dam'd rebel you, what have you been a doing to my wife, you dam'd black scoundrel you? My answer was as quick as possible to him—I have been doing nothing; but that did not seem to be any satisfaction to him, and then I had to spring for a rock as quick as possible, or he would split me through with the hoe.

Aaron was traveling the other side of the Juniata river. I fell in to a white lady's house, and was almost starved to death. She was a tall slim lady, and fair complected, and I asked her for a piece of bread and meat, and she filled my hat full. ' Aaron thinks she had a fair heart too,' for because she done as God commanded her to do. And how was that? To divide with your brethren; and Aaron set down alongside of the Juniata river in the State of Pennsylvania, and begin to eat out of my hat, and Aaron saw a white man come along' "ha," says he, " ye dam'd scoundrel you, get up and come to me." I got up as soon as I could, but I had no idea of coming to him. I stood and considered, and he told me to lay down my hat and come quick—but I laid for the water as quick as possible, and Aaron came across the water; and some places the water took me up to my neck, and the wind blew very hard, and took off my hat, and my bread, and good nice meat with my hat sailed down the river. I consider all that nothing; but the Lord took care of my unworthy life and saved me from drowning, and not only that, but kept my body out of the hands of that Arab, and in the evening Aaron crawled into a barn, and the Lord took care of my unworthy body in that barn, as well as the king in his palace, with his army of soldiers around him. What a blessed thing it is for any poor soul to put their trust in the Lord. The Lord has took care of Aaron through sorrow and affliction; the Lord has delivered me out of the hands of a hard task-master, he has blessed my unworthy body on free soil, and my face Zionward towards his holy kingdom. Since Aaron has come away from my hard task-master, I have fell among sincere Christian people. Sometimes I think I never will have grace to meet these dear friendly white people in heaven. Know that the day's coming that the slaveholder and the slave has got to stand before the tribunal bar, and there render account before a holy God; the same as the murderer stretched on the gallows before judges and jurors. When we are brought before a holy God, whose judgment is quick and powerful, sharper than a two edged sword; his judgment is not like man's, from 30 to 50 years, his judgments are forever. Whilst thousands of years roll around. If we die in the full triumph of a holy faith, we'll take a leap right into his holy kingdom, and there will live forever. And if we die with our hearts shut with sin and iniquity, we'll go down to hell and there will burn forever.

When Aaron was in the town of Kennebunk, in the State of Maine I fell in there with a white friend, he treated Aaron hospitably and got up a meeting for me before I left the place. There was a white gentleman asked me if I knew a man by the name of Ward Richards, a dam'd scoundrel in West Bridgewater. I told him I knew no such person, but I knew a Christian gentleman by the name of Ward Richards. Do you know what the Bible says, if you don't like your brother you must not persecute him.

Aaron thinks you are as destitute of the Bible, and every other good moral principle, or else you would not stand up and persecute your white brother who has done you no harm, because he stands up for equal rights for the poor degraded down trodden African man.

When Aaron was in Princeton, he fell in a white lady's house and I got conversing with her about one thing and another, and she told Aaron of a lady about sixty years of age, and she was always very bitter against the anti-slavery cause. They had an anti-slavery meeting in the place, one of the anti-slavery women went and conversed with this old lady and she got very angry with this anti-slavery woman, and she told her if five cents would free all the negroes in the south, she would not give it. She was knitting as usual about four days afterwards when she fell down dead, and some think it was a judgment of the Almighty upon her for her wicked bad doings.

Since Aaron has left home, I have traveled through about all the free States. I have been mobbed in a great many places, but thank God I have not had any bones broke. His life has been threatened, but my Heavenly Father has looked down from above and saved my unworthy life. I have been highly threatened to be sent back to my hard task-master. Old Beelzebub, the father of sin and iniquity, if he had his way Aaron would have been sent back to his hard task-master long ago. Thank God that God is above the devil, and he has kept Aaron's unworthy body out of the hands of his hard task-master. This is what the way-faring Aaron requested me to write. An abolitionist of Leominster.

THE WORN OUT SLAVE.

A preacher traveling through the Southern States, was rowed across a ferry by a pious old negro who had labored hard through early manhood and middle age to purchase freedom for himself and his wife; and he mourned that old age and loss of strength would compel him to leave all his children in slavery. He laid his hand on his breast, and said, "Master has all my strength, and I have these old bones."

l.
ed
her
her
eled
ght, if
in her
ner cold

es became
orm on her
bile all day
no beds, and
misery when
y drove them
she grieved so
ry time the tra-
it' with dreadful

"She was at length seized with a burning fever, and the trader, fearing he should lose her, carried her the remainder of the way in a wagon.

"When they arrived at Natchez they were all offered for sale, and as Mary was still sick, she begged that she might be sold to a kind master. She sometimes made this request in presence of purchasers—but was always insulted for it, and after they were gone the trader punished her for such presumption in revealing her sickness, and thus preventing her sale. On one occasion he tied her up by her hands so that she could only touch the end of her toes to the floor. This was soon after breakfast; he kept her thus suspended, whipping her at intervals through the day—at evening he took her down. She was so much bruised that she could not lie down for more than a week afterwards."

The rest of her history while a slave is full of horror. Her case differs little from thousands, except that she escaped to reveal her woes, while they suffer and die unheard.

The despatches to the Secretary of War assert that there were in the fort 300 negroes, men, women, and children, and 20 Indians!

The fascinations of an "almost" impenetrable swamp." In 1837, the New Orleans Picayune, reporting the capture of a leader of fugitives, called Squire the "Brigand of the Swamp." While they can support a gang and have a camp, we may expect our negroes to run away. In the same article he says the place whose delight had kept "Squire so long" from the happiness of slavery, and to which the "happy" slaves would of course escape, was a marsh, "almost impenetrable to our citizens." During our two wars with Great Britain, a multitude of slaves fled from their masters and joined the British forces. To furnish the reader some data for judging of the number that escaped during the Revolutionary war, we insert the following extract from Ramsay's History: When the British evacuated Charleston, S. C., in 1782, Governor Matthews demanded the restoration of some thousand of negroes who were within their lines. These, however, were but a small part of the whole taken away at the evacuation, but that number is very inconsiderable when compared with the thousands that were lost from the first to the last of the war. It has been computed by good judges that between the years 1775 and 1783, the State of South Carolina lost twenty-five thousand negroes. See page 30, Ramsay's Hist. S. C., vol. 1. p. 473. At least a fifth part of all the slaves in the State at the beginning of the war. Dr. Ramsay being a native and resident of Charleston, S. C., enjoyed every facility for ascertaining the facts in the case; but his testimony does not stand alone. Col. Lee of Va., in his "Memoirs of the war in the South Department," vol. 2, p. 456, says, of "the negroes seduced and taken from the inhabitants of S. C."—It is asserted upon the authority of the best informed citizens of S. C. that twenty thousand slaves were lost to the State in consequence of the war.

Lord Dunmore, Governor of Virginia, after escaping from Williamsburg in 1775, in a vessel in James River, offered liberty to those slaves who would join him. It appears from the history that one hundred of them are soon after enumerated among his forces. How many joined him does not appear. Burke's Va. vol. 3, p. 431.

Extract of a letter from Mr. Jefferson, then Secretary of State, to Mr. Hammond, minister of Great Britain, dated Philadelphia, Dec. 15, 1791: "On withdrawing the troops from New York, a large embarkation of Negroes, the property of the inhabitants of the U. S., took place. * * * A very great number was carried off in private vessels, without admitting the inspection of the American Commissioners. See "Political correspondence," papers relative to Great Britain, p. 4.

The following may enable the reader to form some judgment of the number that escaped during the last war. Extract from the Report of the committee of Ways and Means, to the House of Representatives, Jan. 5, 1819: "At the conclusion of the war in 1815, it being known that many thousands of the slaves of our citizens had been carried off by the British ships of war," &c.—Am. St. Pap. J. Rel. vol. 4, p. 114. Extract from a letter from Hon. John Quincy Adams to Lord Castlereigh, Feb. 19, 1819. "In his letter of the 5th of Sept., the undersigned had the honor of enclosing a list of 702 slaves carried away after the ratification of the Treaty of Peace from Cumberland Island, and the waters adjacent; * * * * in number perhaps still greater was carried away from Tangier Island in the State of Virginia, and from other states. Am. St. Pap., Id. Sess. 16th Cong., No. 82, p. 82.

There were at Natches on the plantations, a considerable number of negroes, nearly all of whom had joined the murderers of their masters in order to gain their freedom, and had followed their new friends among the Chickasaws. This circumstance and their consequent emancipation were known to their former companions, and suggested the possibility of their own release from bondage. They became restless and indocile. Martin's history of Lo. v. 1. p. 292, date 1832. This property was heretofore but of little value near the Ohio river, because runaways receive aid and protection from the people in the new Territories and States. This was the speech of Doddridge in V. Con. Oct. 28, 1829—Dec. 17, 1831, "Mr. Wright of Maryland laid before the House an attested copy of a resolution passed Feb. 16, 1831, by the General Assembly of the State, complaining of the protection afforded by the citizens of Pennsylvania to the slaves, who abscond and go into that State, and calling for an act of Congress to prevent the continuance of the evils complained of. They say that the present state of things (protection given to the 'happy' fugitives,) is not only vexatious to the master but *extremely pernicious, and calculated to destroy the contentment and happiness* of slaves. "Contented" slaves bad property. Their vicinity to non-slaveholding States, must forever render this sort of property precarious and insecure. Speech of Judge Upshur in the Va. Conv., Oct. 28. 1829.—See Deb. Va. Conv. p. 76.— "From the vicinity of the country through which this, (the Chesapeake and Ohio Canal) passes to Pennsylvania, slaves cannot be held there," Speech of Mr. Scott in the Va. Convention, 1829, Deb. p. 126.

Contentment of Judge Washington's Slaves. Hon. Bushrod Washington, nephew of Gen. Washington, and Judge of the Supreme Court of the U. S., sold 54 of his slaves, to be taken to Louisiana in August, 1831, while he was President of the American Colonization Society. In a letter published in the Baltimore Telegraph, Sept. 18, 1831, he says—"I called the slaves together, and assured them I had no intention to give freedom to any of them. That the *disappointment* caused by this declaration should lead to the consequence which followed *was to be expected.* * * * I had good reason for anticipating the escape of *all the laboring men of any value to the Northern States as soon as I could leave home.*"

Slaves know when to seem contented. Testimony of James Bradley, an emancipated slave:—He bought his freedom in 1832, when nearly 30 years old. In an account of his life in the "Oasis," speaking on this point, he says:— "I do not believe there ever was a slave who did not long for liberty. * * * I was never acquainted with a slave however well he was treated, who did not long to be free. There is one thing about this that people in the free States do not understand. When they ask slaves whether they wish for liberty, they answer "No," and very likely they would say, they would not leave their master for the world. But at the same time, they desire liberty more than any thing else. The truth is, if a slave shows any discontent, he is sure to be treated worse, and worked the harder for it; and every slave knows this. When they are alone, all their talk is about liberty—liberty! It is the great thought and feeling that fills the mind all the time." So Aaron says.

ISAIAH, ch. 59.—A short chapter that the wayfaring Aaron took out of God's holy word.

1. Behold, the Lord's hand is not shortened, that it cannot save; neither is his ear heavy, that it cannot hear:

2. But your iniquities have separated between you and your God, and your sins have hid his face from you, that he will not hear.

3. For your hands are defiled with blood, and your fingers with iniquity; your lips have spoken lies, your tongue hath muttered perverseness.

4. None calleth for justice, nor any pleadeth for truth: they trust in vanity and speak lies; they conceive mischief, and bring forth iniquity.

5. They hatch cockatrice's eggs, and weave the spider's web: he that eateth of their eggs dieth, and that which is crushed breaketh out into a viper.

6. Their webs shall not become garments, neither shall they cover themselves with their works: their works are works of iniquity, and the act of violence is found in their hands.

7. Their feet run to evil, and they make haste to shed innocent blood: their thoughts are thoughts of iniquity; wasting and destruction are in their paths.

8. The way of peace they know not; and there is no judgment in their goings: they have made them crooked paths: Whosoever goeth therein shall not know peace.

9. Therefore is judgment far from us, neither doth justice overtake us: We wait for light, but behold obscurity; for brightness, but we walk in darkness.

10. We grope for the wall like the blind, and we grope as if we had no eyes: we stumble at noon-day as in the night; we are in desolate places as dead men.

11. We roar all like bears, and mourn sore like doves: we look for judgment, but there is none; for salvation, but it is far off from us.

12. For our transgressions are multiplied before thee, and our sins testify against us; and as for our iniquities, we know them.

13. In transgressing and lying against the Lord, and departing away from our God, speaking oppression and revolt, conceiving and uttering from the heart words of falsehood.

14. And judgment is turned away backward, and justice standeth afar off: for truth is fallen in the street, and equity cannot enter.

15. Yea, truth faileth; and he that departeth from evil maketh himself a prey: and the Lord saw it, and it displeased him that there was no judgment.

16. And he saw that there was no man, and wondered that there was no intercessor; therefore his arm brought salvation unto him; and his righteousness, it sustained him.

17. For he put on righteousness as a breastplate, and an helmet of salvation upon his head; and he put on the garments of vengeance for clothing, and was clad with zeal as a cloak.

18. According to their deeds, accordingly he will repay; fury to his adversaries, recompense to his enemies; to the islands he will repay recompense.

19. So shall they fear the name of the Lord from the west, and his glory from the rising of the sun. When the enemy shall come in like a flood, the spirit of the Lord shall lift up a standard against him.

20. And the Redeemer shall come to Zion, and unto them that turn from transgression in Jacob, saith the Lord.

21. As for me, this is my covenant with them, saith the Lord; My spirit that is upon thee, and my words which I have put in thy mouth, shall not depart out of thy mouth, nor out of the mouth of thy seed, nor out of the mouth of thy seed's seed saith the Lord, from henceforth and forever.

A section from the Life of Moses Grandy, late a slave:

When I reached Deep Creek, I went to the house of Captain Edward Minner. He was very glad to see me, for in former days I had done much business for him; he said how sorry he had been to hear that I was at field work. He inquired where I was going. I said, to Norfolk, to get some of the merchants to let me have money to buy myself. He replied, ' What did I always say to you? Was it not, that I would let you have the money at any time if you would only tell me when you could be sold?' He called Mrs. Minner into the room, and told her I could be sold for my freedom, she was rejoiced to hear it. He said, 'Put up your horse at Mr. Western's tavern, for you need go no farther; I have plenty of old rusty dollars, and no man shall put his hand on your collar again to say you are a slave. Come and stay with me to-night, and in the morning I will get Mr. Garret's horse, and go with you.'

Next morning we set off, and found master at Major Farrence's, at the cross canal, where I knew he was to be that day, to sell his share of the canal. When I saw him he told me to go toward home, for he would not sell me. I felt sick and sadly disappointed. Captain Minner stepped up to him, and showed him the paper he had given me, saying, 'Mr. Sawyer, is not this your hand-writing?' He replied, 'Mistress said, the last word when I came away, I was not to sell him, but send him home again.' Captain Minner said, 'Mind, gentlemen, I do not want him for a slave; I want to buy him for freedom. He will repay me the money, and I shall not charge him a cent of interest for it. I would not have a colored person to drag me down to hell, for all the money in the world. A gentleman who was by said it was a shame I should be so treated; I had bought myself so often that Mr. Sawyer ought to let me go. The very worst man as an overseer over the persons employed in digging the canal, Mr. Wiley M'Pherson, was there; he was never known to speak in favor of a colored person; even he said that Mr. Sawyer ought to let me go, as I had been sold so often. At length Mr. Sawyer consented I should go for $650, and would take no less. I wished Captain Minner to give the extra $50, and not stand about it. I believe it was what M'Pherson said that induced my master to let me go; for he was well known for his great severity to colored people; so that after even he had said so, master could not stand out. The Lord must have opened M'Pherson's heart to say it.

I have said that M'Pherson was an overseer where slaves were employed in cutting canals. The labor there is very severe. The ground is often very boggy; the negroes are up to the middle, or much deeper, in mud and water, cutting away roots and baling out mud; if they can keep their heads above water, they work on. They lodge in huts, or, as they are called, camps, made of shingles or boards. They lie down in the mud which has adhered to them, making a great fire to dry themselves, to keep off the cold. No bedding whatever is allowed them; it is only by work done over his task that any of them can get a blanket. They are paid nothing, except for this over-work. Their masters come once a month to receive the money for their labor: then, perhaps, some few very good masters will give them $2 each, some others $1, some a pound of tobacco, and some nothing at all. The food is more abundant than that of field slaves: indeed, it is the best allowance in America—it consists of a peck of meal and six pounds of pork per week; the pork is commonly not good; it is damaged, and is bought as cheap as possible, at auction.

M'Pherson gave the same task to each slave; of course the weak ones often failed to do it. I have often seen him tie up persons and flog them in the morning, only because they were unable to get the previous day's task done; after they were flogged, pork or beef brine was put on their bleeding backs to increase the pain; he sitting by, resting himself, and seeing it done. After being thus flogged and pickled, the sufferers often remained tied up all day, the feet just touching the ground, the legs tied, and pieces of wood put between the legs. All the motion allowed was a slight turn of the neck.—Thus exposed and helpless, the yellow flies and musquitoes in great numbers would settle on the bleeding and smarting back, and put the sufferer to extreme torture. This continued all day, for they were not taken down till night.

---

1. Christ died a martyr, so shall I,
Of my own death I prophecy.
I shall be kill'd for God and Truth,
I have it from the Lord's own mouth.

2. When many years are passed away,
My death 's decreed unto a day;
But where and when I cannot tell,
Till God the same to me reveal.

3. I'm sure he will a token give
Before the blow I shall receive,
That man's not born shall shed my blood.
I have it from the mouth of God.

4. But soon he shall, to grow a man,
As it's in God, Jehovah's plan.
My blood it must and shall be shed,
He shall be born to do the deed.

5. His birth's at hand, shall be this year,*
As days to come shall make it clear;
This gives me no uneasiness,
Not when nor where my death takes place.

6. God by it shall be glorified,
With my own blood my clothes be dy'd,
And with it seal the precious truth,
The Holy Ghost brings through my mouth.

---

* Composed Tuesday Morning, September the 16th, 1828, New York.

When I had composed the hymn, I wrote it in my book now before me. When I had wrote it, I soon forgot it, till on the morning of Dec. 29, 1828, before 12 o'clock, as I had been in bed two hours and could not sleep, I heard a voice say, Arise and pray. I did not the first nor second time get up, till the third time I could not resist. I got out of bed, put on my cloak, and kneeled by my bedside. The clock struck 12. I was one hour in prayer. When the clock struck one, I rose from my knees and got into bed; my head was scarcely on my pillow, when it was spoke to my soul, The child is born shall shed thy blood. The power was so great, I got out of bed, struck a light, and sat down and wrote the six verses. So the child was then born to shed my blood; he was 16 years of age December 29, 1844. Peter knew he should be put to death long before it took place.

The child is born shall shed your blood,
  Commit thy death to me
Before you die shall see his face,
  I'll show him unto thee.

Fear not my son thy glory's sure,
  In death shall feel no pain;
It is my will thy precious blood
  Shall thy own body stain.

Thy blood shall witness to the world,
  The truth brought from thy mouth,
To spread thy fame when thou art dead,
  I have decreed thy death.

Be of good cheer, I am thy God,
  My love is great to thee;
And by thy death, and in that way
  I glorified will be.

You have the saints before you gone,
  Whose blood was freely shed.
I will be with thee in your death,
  Then what have you to dread?

Rejoice my son, nor be afraid,
  Commit thy death to me;
You'll have no time to feel a pain,
  So sud en it shall be.

Composed Monday morning, December 29th, 1828, New York, by Jonathan Cossington, preacher of God's Word, in our house in Malden, Mass., near Boston. Paul preached in his hired house, I in our own house every Lord's day. I want no high steeple house to preach in, and not paid for.

1. Despisest thou a color'd man?
  Then thou despisest God.
They are this day, I will confess,
  Jehovah's flesh and blood.

2. As dear to him as God's dear Son,
  Lov'd and redeem'd by blood,
Dare we despise and set at naught
  Those people dear to God?

3. My God, remove your prejudice,
  And turn your hate to love,
And then through God's great love and
  His blessing you shall prove. [grace,

4. And with them join to bless the Lord
  And love them as thyself.

I'm bound to love and honor God,
  And plead on their behalf.

5. And that to my last drop of blood,
  If God will have it so.
I'm not afraid, if I am call'd,
  Into a prison go.

6. A colored man, through God the
  The Prophet's cause to plead, [means
Up from the dungeon he was drawn,
  And from his prison free'd.

7. That color'd man was blest of God,
  He made his life his care,
And with the saints in Glory, he
  Be sure he hath his share.

Composed Monday Noon, June the 17th, 1844.

Portland city, Tuesday, June, 18. We went to the great Market Hall to hear the speeches of those who should speak on the Abolition of Slavery. One man spoke near an hour, and when he had done, a gentleman said it is free for any one to speak. I went on the platform and said, I am not ashamed to entertain a colored man and feed him at our table. Me and my wife have had them sit with us and eat and drink, as many in Boston and Cambridge can bear witness to, and in Philadelphia and New York, where I have preached to hundreds of colored people in Anthony street, New York, for Benjamin Paul. Let me say to you that despise a colored person, you despise God and his image. I am willing to suffer with them and for them, when I am called to; yes, to prison and death, if it was or should be a law so made, to eat and drink with a black man at my table. Poor despised Aaron has eat and drunk with me and my wife at our own table this supper time; we have read with him and prayed with and for him, and now he is in bed; yes, our best bed, with clean sheets and plenty of covering. This night, March 13th, 1845, Malden, he asked me to write him the seven verses; I have, and am now writing while he is in bed and asleep to rest his wearied body. He called here last Friday, the 7th, and we bought one of his books. We love poor Aaron; let who may despise him, we do not. I said when I had read the seven verses in the Hall in Portland, find me a congregation of poor colored people and send for me, and I am willing to spend and be spent among them, and my wife is willing to go and teach the children to read, and the girls to sew. [*Cheers.*] I was 71 the 6th of this month, in good health, as able to preach as ever, 3 sermons on Lord's days. May the Lord bless poor Aaron and his wife, and all who love Jesus Christ, white or black. I am Jonathan Cossington, the old rough, crooked, and tough ram's horn, whom all hell cant straighten, nor plane, nor break. A ram's horn is crooked, and men nor devils cant make it straight; it is rough, and men cant plane it; it is tough, and men cant break it, lay what burdens you will upon it. So are God's beloved, chosen and called, and made faithful ministers. God's ministers are burden bearers, and the Lord bears with all his people, the true church of God, not the synagogue of Satan. I preached 3 years and 8 months in Christy street school, and all I received did not amount to $400. For these last 13 years I have had only six dollars for 3 sermons. I preached in 1835 in Philadelphia, at Sanson street. God gave me sons and daughters in New York, whom I baptized in the great East river, before thousands of people. Me and my wife have 5 dollars weekly to live. This house is our own bought and paid for. God has given me a godly wife. Under God, as the means in his hands, I preached 8 sermons in April, 1831. She came to hear; and in the next year, July the 29th, 1832, we were married in her own house in Purchase street, by Dr. Jenks, and I preached the same evening to a great room full of people. But we now live in Malden. We have bought this house, and live here, and let our house in Boston, Mass. Saints, white or black, that come this way, call at our house and you shall see plain wholesome food before you set, then blest and sanctified of God, we'll say, beloved friends sit down and eat. The clock has struck ten some time; I must lay down my pen and go to my bed; and dear Aaron, he doth lay up stairs, over our bedroom below. Lord, make our sleep sweet, and keep us from all evil. Amen and Amen.

Aaron's old master used to buy two and a half pounds of butter, and that amount had to last two weeks; and if it did not last two weeks, he used to give all the slaves a puke, and whichever throwed up bread and butter used to have to take a hard whipping on the naked back.

Aaron says a black man can live at the south for one dollar a month, as well as he can live at the north for five; and if the blacks were all set free, they would be troubled with but a very few at the north.

The following facts occurred early in 1844. The brig Henry, on her return from Africa, laden with 400 Africans, was overtaken and hailed by a man of war. Refusing to surrender, a short conflict ensued, in which the captain fell, shot through the body, and fell overboard. The crew then surrendered. The poor Africans were taken on board the man of war, and carried back to their own land, and set at liberty. The author received this account from Mr. Lee of Boston, an eye witness.

AARON'S HOME.

Aaron lives in Springfield, a mile and a half from the Connecticut river, in a little red house, one story high, situated upon the 'Hill.' Throw in your mite to help on the wayfaring Aaron, because he is honest and true.

Aaron says slavery is a load of grief, but freedom is a load of joy.

The Lord is a sun and shield. He will give grace and glory, and no good thing will he withhold from them that walk uprightly. The wayfaring Aaron.

When Aaron was in Bolton he says he called at a lady's house, and she locked the door against him, and then she went and drew back the curtains, and stuck up her nose at him, and then she went and told the neighbors she was afraid of him, a lying trollope.

The slaveholder says that the "negroes" are not worth any thing. Aaron who has been a slave, has informed me, and says, when a slave has been away ten years, if his master can get him, he will take him. Aaron says that the slave holders say every thing but their prayers; those they never say, from the heart, but they say them from the head, because if they said them from the heart, they would not live in sin in the manner they do.

When Aaron was in Rhode Island, I put up at a house among some colored brethren, and there was some very fine colored women lived there. But there was one who had a child by a white man; and she told Aaron that she would sooner have a child by a white man than by a 'nigger.' Aaron is astonished when I see colored women so foolish, especially in a free land; because one half of the white men don't consider the colored people human.

A tribute from Aaron to Rhode Island.

There is what they call the 'Suffrage party,' and the 'Algerine party' in Rhode Island; the 'Suffrage party' tells Aaron that they are in the very greatest kind of bondage. I have traveled all through Rhode Island state, and I don't see any whipping posts there; and when Aaron strikes into Providence, I don't see any "VALUABLE PEOPLE FOR SALE," the way I do when I get into Richmond, Virginia; they put up "VALUABLE NEGROES FOR SALE TO DAY." And I don't see any man and wife parted in Rhode Island state, who has been living together for 18 or 19 years, and reared up a family of children. They aint sold one way, and the children sold another; and they aint drove into the mills to work with a whip, the way the poor blacks are drove into the potatoe and tobacco fields, and every time they don't do just so, they are hit twenty or thirty lashes on the naked back, and dare not open their heads. It is not so in Rhode Island state with the Suffrage party. When they do their labor, instead of getting their pay on the back, they get it in the hand. Aaron thinks if they were situated the way of the poor African, in old Virginia, then I would consider them slaves; but they are not situated so. Aaron says that one half of these men who are in such bondage in Rhode Island, care nothing about their poor African brethren, who are in a great deal worse bondage than they are.

DREAMS.—Aaron is a firm believer in dreams. If you dream of a wedding, you need not feed yourself with the idea that you are going to get married. Prepare yourself to die, to meet your God in a coming day.—MR. JAMES PAINE.

Aaron's health is very poor, and he is sick two-thirds of the time; and this is the only way he has to make an honest living; and I think it is traveling about that keeps him alive.

> Angels assist our mighty joys,
> Strike all your harps of gold;
> But when you raise your highest notes
> His love can ne'er be told.

Here is a short sentence of Dr. Watts, who suffered heavy persecution on ight hand and on the left, but by the assistance of a holy God he won great battle, and is now shining in his Master's kingdom.

"In vain thou strugglest to get free,
I never will unloose my hold."

This is the way the slaveholder is continually grasping the slave. Lord, have mercy upon the poor slaveholder. May he hear the rumbling of Jehovah's chariot wheels, like seven-fold peals of thunder to the awakening of his ungodly soul.

Here is a short sentence the wayfaring Aaron requested me to write out of his own head.

Behold the good judgment of his mind, being reared up in slavery. It's enough to astonish a nation. Aaron is sometimes up and sometimes down; but like the old pilgrim, freighted with grace and bound for heaven.

"The Lord is my Shepherd, I shall not want. He maketh me to lie down in green pastures; he leadeth me beside still waters.

He restoreth my soul; he leadeth me in the paths of righteousness for his name's sake. Yea, though I walk through the valley of the shadow of death I will fear no evil, for thou art with me; thy rod and thy staff they comfort me.

Thou preparest a table before me in the presence of mine enemies; thou anointest my head with oil; my cup runneth over.

Surely goodness and mercy shall follow me all the days of my life; and I will dwell in the house of the Lord forever.

That is the way with the christian who has enlisted under the blood-stained banner of king Immanuel.

Isaiah 3d Chapter.

10. Say ye to the righteous, that it shall be well with him: for they shall eat the fruit of their doings.

11. Woe unto the wicked! it shall be ill with him: for the reward of his hands shall be given him.

12. As for my people, my children are their oppressors, and women rule over them. O my people, they which lead thee cause thee to err, and destroy the way of thy paths.

13. The Lord standeth up to plead, and standeth to judge the people.

14. The Lord will enter into judgment with the ancients of his people, and the princes thereof: for ye have eaten up the vineyard; the spoil of the poor is in your houses.

15. What mean ye that ye beat my people to pieces, and grind the faces of the poor? saith the Lord God of hosts.

16. Moreover the Lord saith, Because the daughters of Zion are haughty, and walk with stretched forth necks and wanton eyes, walking and mincing as they go, and making a tinkling with their feet:

17. Therefore the Lord will smite with a scab the crown of the head of the daughters of Zion, and the Lord will discover their secret parts.

18. In that day the Lord will take away the bravery of their tinkling ornaments about their feet, and their cauls, and their round tires like the moon.

19. The chains, and the bracelets, and the mufflers,

20. The bonnets, and the ornaments of the legs, and the headbands, and the tablets, and the earrings,

21. The rings, and nose jewels,

22. The changeable suits of apparel, and the mantles, and the wimples, and the crisping pins,

23. The glasses, and the fine linen, and the hoods, and the veils.

24. And it shall come to pass, that instead of sweet smell there shall be stink; and instead of a girdle a rent; and instead of well set hair baldness; and instead of a stomacher a girding of sackcloth; and burning instead of beauty.

25. Thy men shall fall by the sword, and thy mighty in the war.

26. And her gates shall lament and mourn; and she being desolate shall sit upon the ground.

Old Beelzebub, the father of sin and iniquity, he tempted me till I like to loose my soul in iniquity, but blessed Michael helped me out of my distress, and armed me with the sword and shield, to march for Canaan's land. Sweet fields arrayed in living green, and rivers of delight; no chilling winds nor poisonous breath can reach that happy shore; glittering crowns and glaring swords will there our armies be. We'll sing and shout forevermore, around our father's throne.

ISAIAH, 5th chp. 10, 18, 20.—Woe unto them that rise up early in the morning, that they may follow strong drink; that continue until wine inflame them. Woe unto them that draw iniquity with cords of vanity, and sin as it were with a cart rope. Woe unto them that call evil good, and good evil; that put darkness for light and light for darkness; that put bitter for sweet, and sweet for bitter. This is the way Aaron thinks it is with the christian(?) slaveholders at the south, who call themselves angels. He that takes one letter out of God's holy word, his part is taken out of the kingdom; so Aaron says. And he says that a white minister will not own a colored minister at the south if be can help it, for they say that they preach and spoil all the negroes.

>What pain, what labor, he's secured
>My soul to endless rest.

Aaron is a firm believer in witchcraft. The way to fortify yourselves against it is by faith and humble prayer. We read in God's holy word, that with his chariot wheels he drags all the powers of hell. That is the reason why Aaron thinks that by carrying three horse-shoe nails in his right pocket he may overcome them.

When Aaron lived in Lancaster, Ohio, he got acquainted with an old lady who told him she was acquainted with a man who lived there, and used to hire a great many black persons to work for him. He was always very bitter against the blacks' having their freedom. The man and his wife died. They had three children, and they all came to naught, and lived day after day among the blacks, because the whites would not take them in.

Aaron is acquainted with a young woman who told him she was well acquainted with a young man who sold a colored man three times in the south, and agreed to pay the colored man one-half of the money he got for him; and the last time he sold him, he asked him to ride with him by the side of a river, and he then slipped behind the colored man and blew his brains out, and then cut him open, took out his lights, and sunk him in the deep for the sake of his money. Aaron thinks that a holy God will sink him in a dying hour in the same way.

Aaron says some shallow professors are always praying that sin and trouble may be removed out of the land, but never do anything to remove it themselves, and think to sail to heaven on flowery beds of ease.

I asked a man of sorrows, and of tears,
Whose looks told anguish pressed him more than years;
He mused awhile, and then distinctly said—
" Life is a burden—would that I were dead."

I asked a Christian, who had early strayed
From virtue's paths; this was the answer made—
" Life is a precious boon to mortals given,
Which, if well spent, will be renewed in heaven.'

Here is a short sentence of Aaron's.

Give a child an apple in each hand; set four apples down on the table, and it will cry for the four. Aaron thinks the slaveholders are something like this greedy child. There are a great many slaveholders who say they pity poor slaves. To hear them talk, you would think that butter would not melt in their mouths; but Aaron says those very same men would knock a slave in the head if he but crooked his finger at them. Aaron thinks that slavery ought to be abolished, if they do, plaster it up and call it domestic. It is a dark sin in the sight of a holy God.

I lodge awhile in tents below,
I gladly wander to and fro,
    Till I my Canaan gain.

Here is a short sentence of the wayfaring Aaron. How true it is, brethren.

By prayer let me wrestle, and he will perform;
With Christ in the vessel, I smile at the storm.

Here is a short sentence of the way-faring Aaron.

Here I go to be baptized,   Silver slippers on my feet,
By my Lord to be baptized,   And a golden girdle round my waist,
Sing Glory, sing Glory   Sing glory, sing glory,
    And honor to the Lamb.   And honor to the Lamb.

Down to the pool to be baptized,
By my Lord to be baptized,
Here is water enough to be baptized
By my Lord to be baptized.
Sing glory, sing glory, and honor to the Lamb.

That's the way it is with the Christian, when his warfare is ended here below. Here is a short sentence of the wayfaring Aaron.

Here is a short sentence of Aaron's, in conclusion:
Good News and Glad Tidings and Great Joy. — He that is free in Christ is free indeed. Then this is heaven; I have often heard of heaven. Behold here it is !— Broad is the road that leads to death, and thousands walk together there; but wisdom shows a narrow path, with here and there a traveler.